TOWARD PEER LEADERSHIP AS A HIGH-IMPACT PRACTICE

INSIGHTS FROM THE U.S. DATA IN THE 2023 INTERNATIONAL SURVEY OF PEER LEADERS

Bryce Bunting and Dallin George Young, Editors

Research Report No.

13

Cite as:

Bunting, B. D., & Young, D. G. (Eds.). (2024). *Toward peer leadership as a high-impact practice: Insights from the U.S. data in the 2023 International Survey of Peer Leaders*. University of South Carolina, National Resource Center for The First-Year Experience & Students in Transition.

ISBN: 978-1-942072-77-5 (paperback)
ISBN: 978-1-942072-78-2 (epub)
ISBN: 978-1-942072-79-9 (ebrary)

Library of Congress Control Number: 2024952573
Published by:
National Resource Center for The First-Year Experience® and Students in Transition
University of South Carolina
Carolina Coliseum, 701 Assembly Street, Suite 1000, Columbia, SC 29201
www.sc.edu/fye

Production Staff for the National Resource Center:

Design and Production:	Jenna A. Seabold, Project Manager
	Sammy Lopez, Graphics Artist
	Stephanie L. McFerrin, Graphic Artist
	Makayla Rippy, Graphic Artist
Reviewers:	Michael Graham, Lander University
	Kathleen J. Lehman, National Resource Center for the First-Year Experience and Students in Transition
	Scotty M. Secrist, Purdue University
	Charmaine E. Troy, Georgia Tech
	Kevin Wenger, National Resource Center for the First-Year Experience and Students in Transition

About the Publisher

The National Resource Center for The First-Year Experience and Students in Transition was born out of the success of the University of South Carolina's much-honored University 101 course and a series of annual conferences focused on the freshman year experience. The momentum created by the educators attending these early conferences paved the way for the development of the National Resource Center, which was established at the University of South Carolina in 1986. As the National Resource Center broadened its focus to include other significant student transitions in higher education, it underwent several name changes, adopting the National Resource Center for The First-Year Experience and Students in Transition in 1998.

Today, the Center collaborates with its institutional partner, University 101 Programs, in pursuit of its mission to advance and support efforts to improve student learning and transitions into and through higher education. We achieve this mission by providing opportunities for the exchange of practical and scholarly information as well as the discussion of trends and issues in our field through convening conferences and other professional development events such as institutes, workshops, and online learning opportunities; publishing scholarly practice books, research reports, a peer-reviewed journal, electronic newsletters, and guides; generating, supporting, and disseminating research and scholarship; hosting visiting scholars; and maintaining several online channels for resource sharing and communication, including a dynamic website, listservs, and social media outlets.

The National Resource Center serves as the trusted expert, internationally recognized leader, and clearinghouse for scholarship, policy, and best practice for all postsecondary student transitions.

Institutional Home

The National Resource Center is located at the University of South Carolina's (USC) flagship campus in Columbia. Chartered in 1801, USC Columbia's mission is twofold: to establish and maintain excellence in its student population, faculty, academic programs, living and learning environment, technological infrastructure, library resources, research and scholarship, public and private support and endowment; and to enhance the industrial, economic, and cultural potential of the state. The Columbia campus offers 324 degree programs through its 15 degree-granting colleges and schools. In fiscal year 2024, faculty generated $309 million in funding for research, outreach, and training programs. USC is among the top tier of universities receiving Research and Community Engagement designations from the Carnegie Foundation.

Contents

Tables and Figures

Tables

Figures

Part 1

Framing the Results: Background and Context of the Report

Chapter 1

Introduction and Overview of the US Administration of the 2023 International Survey of Peer Leaders

Bryce D. Bunting
Brigham Young University

Dallin George Young
University of Georgia

For three decades, educational researchers have investigated the role that peers play in the learning and development that occurs during the college experience. Nearly every theory of student development that emerged during this time has suggested, in one way or another, that students' most meaningful learning occurs as they interact with each other in educationally purposeful activities (e.g., Evans et al., 2009; Mayhew et al., 2016; Skipper, 2005; Tinto, 2012). Researchers have suggested that "interactions with peers [are] probably the most pervasive and powerful force in student persistence and degree completion" (Pascarella & Terenzini, 2005, p. 615). Positive relationships with peers are correlated with student flourishing (Mayhew et al., 2016) and play a critical role in supporting student success (Peregrina-Kretz et al., 2018). It is not surprising, then, that practitioners and researchers continue to cite Astin's (1993) powerful claim about the power of peers: "The student's peer group is the single most potent source of influence on growth and development during the undergraduate years" (p. 398).

Higher education professionals have capitalized on these findings by engaging peer leaders (PLs) in a variety of settings, from academic advising to residence life and from orientation to the senior year experience (Ganser & Kennedy, 2012; Skipper & Keup, 2017). Although the structure and administration of PL programs varies depending on the unique needs and features of a particular college or university, there is a commonality across PL types. The term "peer leader" describes a variety of roles wherein "students who have been selected and trained… offer educational services to their peers … intentionally designed to assist in the adjustment, satisfaction, and persistence of students toward attainment of their educational goals" (Ender & Kay, 2001, p. 1).

At their core all PL programs assume that PLs offer something unique from the support students receive from faculty members and professional staff. As a result, peer leadership has a triple-impact in that it benefits student recipients, the institution, and the PLs themselves (Keup, 2020). The use of PLs provides a range of benefits to student recipients, including strengthened confidence that they can succeed in college, support as they adjust to college life, increased intentions to stay in school and graduate, and allies for sharing personal concerns (Collier, 2015).

The benefits of this practice also extend to the institution. In an age of ever-tightening budgets, PLs offer an economical way of providing personal support to students and extending the reach of professional staff. They provide simpler and more effective channels for disseminating key institutional information to large numbers of students. Finally, because of their proximity to and credibility with their peers, PLs have a more accurate understanding of student perceptions, attitudes, and concerns. When institutions tap into this unique expertise, they can better support students, evaluate institutional efforts, and implement large-scale programming (Newton & Ender, 2010; Shook & Keup, 2012).

A final benefit of peer leadership is the learning, growth, and becoming experienced by PLs themselves. We will leave a deep dive into these benefits for subsequent chapters of this report. Nevertheless, it seems appropriate in this introduction to briefly speak to the comprehensive and wide-ranging nature of the learning gains reported by PLs.

Peer leadership offers rich academic benefits (e.g., Bunting et al., 2012; Colvin & Ashman, 2010; Young et al., 2019; Young & Keup, 2018); deepened interpersonal relationships (e.g., Harmon, 2006; Heys & Wawrzynski, 2013; van der Meer et al., 2019; Young et al., 2023); and strong career preparation (e.g., Brack et al., 2008; Carr et al., 2018; Chilvers & Waghorne, 2018; Good et al., 2000; Scott et al., 2019; Young & Keup, 2018). Most importantly, PL experiences can, under particular circumstances, lead to identity-shifting experiences of becoming that cut across discrete learning domains (e.g., Bunting, 2019; Bunting & Williams, 2017; Lee et al., 2022; van der Meer, et al., 2022). Being a PL is part of a class of experiences that helps students achieve one of the primary purposes of college, which is to shift from externally motivated *student* to internally motivated and lifelong *learner* (Sanders, 2018). This report will focus, specifically, on the experiences of PLs and the benefits they report from serving in this unique role supporting their peers.

Introduction and Overview of the 2023 International Survey of Peer Leaders Report

In 2009, the National Resource Center for the First-Year Experience and Students in Transition conducted a pilot study to gather information on the characteristics of peer leadership programs and the perceived outcomes of the peer leadership experience for students participating as PLs. Results of this pilot survey provided important early insights into the common characteristics of PL roles and programs. However, what became most clear from this small pilot was that the students who were serving as PLs were experiencing significant learning and growth in their roles (Keup & Skipper, 2010).

Consequently, the National Resource Center conducted a larger and more comprehensive study of the state of peer leadership in the United States in 2013 through the 2013 National Survey of Peer Leaders (NSPL). The goals of this study were to (a) better understand the practices and outcomes of students engaged in peer leadership across a national context; (b) facilitate benchmarking for individual institutions and programs; and (c) generate practical insights for strengthening the way institutions recruit, train, and supervise undergraduate PLs. Analysis of these survey data provided the first ever research-based portrait of the state of peer leadership across the U.S. higher education landscape.

Findings from the 2013 NSPL provided compelling evidence that students in PL roles experienced elevated levels of engagement, were very satisfied with their experiences, and developed important skills and abilities valued by both their institutions and future employers (Keup & Young, 2014). Additionally, results of the survey have led to numerous publications on peer leadership; countless conference presentations, workshops, and keynote addresses; and a robust international research project examining the state of peer leadership across the globe.

This pioneering work to investigate peer leadership on U.S. college campuses catalyzed subsequent research on peer leadership, including the development of the first International Survey of Peer Leaders (ISPL), administered from 2014 to 2016 in Australia, Canada, New Zealand, South Africa, and the United Kingdom. In 2023, researchers and thought leaders from around the world engaged in an updated administration of the ISPL and aimed to both build on and extend this research dialogue on peer leadership by:

- Using updated data to facilitate continued institutional and programmatic benchmarking related to the structure and administration of PL programs and the outcomes reported by those who serve as PLs,

- Providing insight into the ways in which the landscape of peer leadership in the United States has shifted since the administration of the NSPL in 2013, and

- Allowing for cross-national comparisons with the other countries participating in the broader ISPL project.

To facilitate administration of the International Survey of Peer Leaders in the United States (ISPL-US), our research team worked to establish partnerships with several prominent professional associations representing key functional areas in higher education that sponsor large numbers of PLs. We used two criteria in our selection of partnering organizations. First, results of the 2013 National Survey of Peer Leaders indicated that the most common PL roles were in student clubs and organizations, residence halls, first-year experience (FYE), campus activities, orientation, academic advising, service-learning, and tutoring (Keup & Young, 2014). Second, the research team of the National Resource Center had previously partnered with professional organizations on research on peer leadership that aligned with these results. Through this process, we identified five partner associations:

- NODA: Association for Orientation, Transition, and Retention in Higher Education
- The Association of College and University Housing Officers – International (ACUHO-I)
- NACADA: The Global Community for Academic Advising
- The International Center for Supplemental Instruction
- The National Association for Campus Activities (NACA)

Partnering with these organizations helped to bring credibility to the ISPL-US study and facilitated valuable access to a wide range of PLs, in diverse roles, from across the United States.

We invited each partner association to distribute a call for participating institutions through their various networks and channels. Through this process, we identified 27 participating institutions who then distributed unique institutional survey links to the peer leaders on their campus. Overall, we distributed the survey to 6,641 students and received 1,531 responses, for an overall response rate of just over 23%.

We have provided additional information regarding the ISPL-US in the appendices. Appendix A includes a more detailed description of the methods for the study. In Appendix B we have provided the full ISPL-US survey instrument. Readers can find a list of all the institutions who participated in the ISPL-US in Appendix C. Finally, we have provided a brief demographic profile of the survey participants in Appendix D.

Goals of the Report

While there is growing evidence of the wide-ranging benefits that result when institutions offer peer leadership experiences to students, it is important that practitioners, institutional leaders, and researchers alike avoid the temptation to assume that all PL experiences are created equal. Our first goal with this report is to interrogate the extent to which peer leadership can be considered a high-impact practice (Bunting, 2020; Keup, 2016). More specifically, our analysis of the ISPL-US data focused on evaluating the extent to which the experiences of PLs in the United States align with the characteristics of high-impact practices (HIPs) and contribute to gains in academic abilities, positive social interactions, and feelings of belonging among PLs.

Our hope is that this volume exploring the current landscape of peer leadership in the United States will help add to this chorus of voices and demonstrate that the impact of the PL experience is highly dependent on the *anatomy* of the experience (Bunting, 2020). By that, we mean that high-impact peer leadership experiences only result when the design, implementation, and assessment of these experiences align with the key characteristics of HIPs identified by Kuh and O'Donnell (2013), namely:

- Performance expectations set at appropriately high levels,
- Significant investment of time and effort by students over an extended period,
- Interactions with faculty and peers about substantive matters,
- Experiences with people and circumstances that differ from those with which students are familiar,
- Frequent, timely, and constructive feedback,

- Periodic, structured opportunities to reflect and integrate learning,
- Opportunities to discover the relevance of learning through real-world applications, and
- Public demonstration of competence.

For example, in what ways do job descriptions or postings for PL positions communicate high expectations for PLs' learning and engagement in their experience? To what extent are PLs investing significant time and effort across their experience? How does the training provided to PLs prepare them to explore diverse perspectives and engage with peers who are quite different from themselves? Are there consistent opportunities for PLs to engage in meaningful, structured reflection or to receive substantive and timely feedback on their work and performance? How can we support PLs in articulating, documenting, or demonstrating the learning and skill development they experience through their leadership experience? Our research team intentionally designed the updated 2023 ISPL-US survey instrument to help answer questions like these and to provide deepened understanding of the current state of peer leadership as it relates to the characteristics of HIPs.

With Kinzie et al. (2021), we assert that, when it comes to HIPs—including peer leadership—labels matter far less than the quality of implementation of a particular practice. Similarly, Finley (2019) has cautioned that the recent fervor surrounding various educational practices du jour can lead to a naïve assumption among some campus leaders, who Finley refers to as "casual adopters" (p. 4), that simply offering these practices will somehow facilitate sustained institutional change and improved student outcomes.

Additionally, as researchers have argued elsewhere (Springer et al., 2018; Zilvinkskis et al., 2023), it is imperative that we find ways to assure full and equitable participation in high impact practices and experiences like peer leadership. This is particularly important in any discussion of HIPs because these educational practices yield significant educational benefits for college students from demographic groups who have historically been excluded and underserved by higher education (Kuh, 2008). Indeed, because we know that practices like peer leadership have a transformative impact upon students who participate, we bear an ethical obligation. First, we must ensure that all students can participate in these experiences. Second, the quality of these experiences must be equitable across various demographic groups that make up the population of college students in the United States. First-generation students, students with financial need, and students from minoritized populations should have access to the same high-quality experiences as their historically privileged peers.

To summarize, this report will focus on exploring a few key questions that have relevance for both practitioners looking to implement, refine, or assess peer leadership programs on their campuses; as well as researchers with an interest in drawing upon findings of the 2023 ISPL-US in their own scholarly work:

- Is peer leadership a HIP in its own right? What evidence do we have to make this claim? How might the PL experience be adapted or refined to provide an experience aligned with the characteristics of HIPs?

- What can we learn from the dataset about the experiences of PLs from historically marginalized and excluded populations? Are students from these populations experiencing similar outcomes as their more privileged peers?

- What are the key trends, emerging issues, and future directions for research about PLs and their experiences that ISPL-US findings help to illuminate?

Organization of the Report

Recognizing that the characteristics of PL experiences are situated within particular contexts and functional roles, we chose to invite authors from each of our partner associations (again, aligning with specific functional areas) to discuss and analyze the findings of the ISPL-US within the context of their particular functional areas.

In Chapter 2, we provide an overall discussion of the general survey findings, with a focus on what the survey results suggest about peer leadership as a HIP and pathway to belonging for an increasingly diverse student population. We also introduce a theoretical framework helpful in evaluating and refining the peer leader experience across a variety of campus types.

Our partner organization colleagues authored Chapters 3 through 8 and discuss findings specific to the functional areas discussed previously. Each of these chapters reviews key ISPL-US findings relative to one of the five functional areas outlined previously. We also encouraged authors to (a) offer practical guidance and clear recommendations for how campuses can provide high-impact and transformative peer leader experiences, (b) discuss emerging trends related to peer leadership in their functional area, and (c) provide direction for future research.

Finally, in Chapter 9, we provide an integrative review of the findings presented throughout the report, with a focus on peer leadership as a HIP. Moreover, we discuss key issues and trends for peer leadership that are illuminated by the findings presented by the contributors, including compensation, employability, and belonging. We conclude by identifying pathways for future research.

References

Astin, A. (1993). *What matters in college? Four critical years revisited.* Jossey-Bass Publishers.

Brack, A. B., Millard, M., & Shah, K. (2008). Are peer educators really peers? *Journal of American College Health, 56*(5), 566-568. https://doi.org/10.3200/JACH.56.5.566-568

Bunting, B. D. (2019). Peer leaders as full participants in the academic work of the institution. *Journal of Peer Learning, 12*(1), 1-4. https://ro.uow.edu.au/ajpl/vol12/iss1/1

Bunting, B. D. (2020). The anatomy of high-impact peer learning experiences. *Journal of Peer Learning, 13*(1), 1-4. https://ro.uow.edu.au/ajpl/vol13/iss1/1

Bunting, B., Dye, B., Pinnegar, S., & Robinson, K. (2012). Understanding the dynamics of peer mentor learning: A narrative study. *Journal of the First-Year Experience & Students in Transition, 24*(1), 61-78.

Bunting, B., & Williams, D. (2017). Stories of transformation: Using personal narrative to explore transformative experience among undergraduate peer mentors. *Mentoring & Tutoring: Partnership in Learning, 25*(2), 166-184. https://doi.org/10.1080/13611267.2017.1327691

Carr, R. A., Evans-Locke, K., Abu-Saif, H., Boucher, R., & Douglas, K. (2018). Peer-learning to employable: Learnings from an evaluation of PASS attendee and facilitator perceptions of employability at Western Sydney University. *Journal of Peer Learning, 11*(1), 41-64. https://ro.uow.edu.au/ajpl/vol11/iss1/4

Chilvers, L., & Waghorne, J. (2018). Exploring PASS leadership beyond graduation. *Journal of Peer Learning, 11*(2), 5-26. https://ro.uow.edu.au/ajpl/vol11/iss1/2

Collier, P. J. (2015). *Developing effective student peer mentoring programs: A practitioner's guide to program design, delivery, evaluation, and training.* Stylus.

Colvin, J. W., & Ashman, M. (2010). Roles, risks, and benefits of peer mentoring relationships in higher education. *Mentoring & Tutoring: Partnership in Leaning, 18*(2), 121-134. https://doi.org/10.1080/13611261003678879

Ender, S. C. & Kay, K. (2001). Peer leader programs: A rationale and review of the literature. In S. L. Hamid (Ed.), *Peer leadership: A primer on program essentials* (Monograph no. 32, pp. 1-12). University of South Carolina, National Resource Center for The First-Year Experience and Students in Transition.

Evans, N. J., Forney, D. S., Guido, F. M., Patton, L. D., & Renn, K. A. (2009). *Student development in college: Theory, research, and practice.* John Wiley & Sons.

Finley, A. (2019, November). A comprehensive approach to assessment of high-impact practices (Occasional Paper No. 41). University of Illinois and Indiana University, National Institute for Learning Outcomes Assessment (NILOA). https://www.learningoutcomesassessment.org/wp-content/uploads/2019/11/Occasional-Paper-41.pdf

Ganser, S. R., & Kennedy, T. L. (2012). Where it all began: Peer education and leadership in student services. *New Directions for Higher Education, 2012*(157), 17-29. https://doi.org/10.1002/he.20003

Good, J. M., Halpin, G., & Halpin, G. (2000). A promising prospect for minority retention: Students becoming peer mentors. *Journal of Negro Education, 69*(4), 375-383. https://doi.org/10.2307/2696252

Harmon, B. N. (2006). A qualitative study of the learning processes and outcomes associated with students who serve as peer mentors. *Journal of The First-Year Experience and Students in Transition, 18*(2), 53-82.

Heys, K. H., & Wawrzynski, M. R. (2013). Male peer educators: Effects of participation as peer educators on college men. *Journal of Student Affairs Research and Practice, 50*(2), 189-207. https://doi.org/10.1515/jsarp-2013-0014

Keup, J. R. (2016). Peer leadership as an emerging high-impact practice: An exploratory study of the American experience. *Journal of Student Affairs in Africa, 4*(1), 33-52. https://doi.org/10.14426/jsaa.v4i1.143

Keup, J. R. (2020). Peer leadership, higher education. In P. N. Teixeira & J. C. Shin (Eds.), *The international encyclopedia of higher education systems and institutions* (pp. 2202-2210). Springer Nature. https://doi.org/10.1007/978-94-017-8905-9

Keup, J. R., & Skipper, T. L. (2010, March 21-24). *Findings from the 2009 National Survey of Peer Leaders* [Conference presentation]. ACPA 2010 Convention, Boston, MA, United States. https://sc.edu/nrc/system/pub_files/1549303973_0.pdf

Keup, J. R., & Young, D. G. (2014, March 30-April 2). *The power of peers: Exploring the impact of peer leader experiences* [Conference presentation]. ACPA 2014 Convention, Indianapolis, IN, United States. https://sc.edu/nrc/system/pub_files/1532454855_0.pdf

Kinzie, J., Silberstein, S., McCormick, A. C., Gonyea, R. M., & Dugan, B. (2021). Centering racially minoritized student voices in high-impact practices. *Change: The Magazine of Higher Learning, 53*(4), 6-14. https://doi.org/10.1080/00091383.2021.1930976

Kuh, G. D. (2008). High-impact educational practices: *What they are, who has access to them, and why they matter.* American Association of Colleges and Universities.

Kuh, G. D., & O'Donnell, K. (2013). *Ensuring quality and taking high-impact practices to scale.* Association of American Colleges and Universities.

Lee, B., Liu, K., Warnock, T. S., Kim, M. O., & Skett, S. (2022). Students leading students: A qualitative study exploring a student-led model for engagement with the sustainable development goals. *International Journal of Sustainability in Higher Education, 24*(3), 535-552. https://doi.org/10.1108/IJSHE-02-2022-0037

Mayhew, M. J., Rockenbach, A. N., Bowman, N. A., Seifert, T. A., & Wolniak, G. C. (2016). *How college affects students: 21st century evidence that higher education works* (Vol. 1). John Wiley & Sons.

Newton, F. B., & Ender, S. C. (2010). *Students helping students: A guide for peer educators on college campuses* (2nd. ed.). John Wiley & Sons.

Pascarella, E. T., & Terenzini, P. T. (2005). *How college affects students: A third decade of research* (Vol. 2). Jossey-Bass.

Peregrina-Kretz, D., Seifert, T., Arnold, C., & Burrow, J. (2018). Finding their way in post-secondary education: The power of peers as connectors, coaches, co-constructors and copycats. *Higher Education Research & Development, 37*(5), 1076-1090. https://doi.org/10.1080/07294360.2018.1471050

Sanders, M. L. (2018). *Becoming a learner: Realizing the opportunity of education.* Hayden-Mcneil.

Scott, C. A., McLean, A., & Golding, C. (2019). *How peer mentoring fosters graduate attributes. Journal of Peer Learning, 12*(3), 29-44. https://ro.uow.edu.au/ajpl/vol12/iss1/3

Shook, J. L., & Keup, J. R. (2012). The benefits of peer leader programs: An overview from the literature. In J. R. Keup (Ed.), *New directions in higher education: Peer leadership in higher education* (no. 157, pp. 5-16). Jossey-Bass. https://doi.org/10.1002/he.20002

Skipper, T. L. (2005). *Student development in the first college year: A primer for college educators.* University of South Carolina, National Resource Center for The First-Year Experience and Students in Transition.

Skipper, T. L., & Keup, J. R. (2017). The perceived impact of peer leadership experiences on college academic performance. *Journal of Student Affairs Research and Practice, 54*(1), 95-108. https://doi.org/10.1080/19496591.2016.1204309

Springer, J. T., Hatcher, J., & Powell, A. (2018). High-impact practices: The call for a commitment to quality educational experiences and inclusive excellence. *Assessment Update, 30*(4), 6–11. https://scholarworks.iupui.edu/server/api/core/bitstreams/a1a3ee0f-48d9-44e5-88c7-7decae4c2a4c/content

Tinto, V. (2012). Leaving college: *Rethinking the causes and cures of student attrition* (2nd ed.). University of Chicago Press.

van der Meer, J., Skalicky, J., & Speed, H. (2019). "I didn't just want a degree": Students' perceptions about benefits from participation in student leadership programmes. *Journal of Leadership Education, 18*(1). https://doi.org/10.12806/V18/I1/R3

van der Meer, J., Skalicky, J., Speed, H., & Young, D. G. (2022). Focusing on the development of the whole student: An international comparative study of the perceived benefits of peer leadership in higher education. *Open Journal of Social Sciences, 10*(3), 14-35. https://doi.org/10.12806/V18/I1/R3

Young, D. G., Hoffman, D. E., & Frakes Reinhardt, S. (2019). An exploration of the connection between participation in academic peer leadership experiences and academic success. *Journal of Peer Learning, 12*(1), 45-60. https://ro.uow.edu.au/ajpl/vol12/iss1/4

Young, D. G., & Keup, J. R. (2018). To pay or not to pay: The influence of compensation as an external reward on learning outcomes of peer leaders. *Journal of College Student Development, 59*(2), 159-176. https://doi.org/10.1353/csd.2018.0015

Young, D. G., Zeng, W., Skalicky, J., & van der Meer, J. (2023). The quality and quantity of participation in peer leader experiences and student outcomes: A cross-national validation of constructs and predictive model. *Research in Higher Education,* 1-21. https://doi.org/10.1007/s11162-023-09765-4

Zilvinskis, J., Kinzie, J., Daday, J., O'Donnell, K., & Zande, C. V. (2022). Introduction: When done well: 14 years of chasing an admonition. In J. Zilvinskis, J. Kinzie, J. Daday, K. O'Donnell, & C. V. Zande (Eds.), *Delivering on the promise of high-impact practices: Research and models for achieving equity, fidelity, impact, and scale* (pp. 1-10). Taylor & Francis. https://doi.org/10.4324/9781003444022-1

Chapter 2

Peer Leadership: A High-Impact Practice that Addresses Contemporary Concerns in Higher Education

Bryce D. Bunting
Brigham Young University

Dallin George Young
University of Georgia

As we discussed how to approach reporting on the findings of the International Survey of Peer Leaders administered in the United States (ISPL-US), we felt drawn to creating a research report that would do more than simply provide readers with access to the data we had collected and our cursory commentary on those data. Early in the research process it became apparent that, like most survey research, we were gathering far more data than we could address in a single report. That said, we have worked to provide relevant and insightful data throughout the body of the report.

However, beyond providing simple access to data, our hope was to engage practitioners, institutional leaders, and researchers in a reflective conversation focused on the powerful potential of peer leadership to promote transformative learning among those students who serve in these varied leadership roles. Also, we saw an opportunity to use the ISPL-US findings to provide insight into how well-designed peer leadership experiences can help address broader contemporary concerns in higher education. This has meant making tough decisions about what to focus on and highlight in the chapters that follow.

As we begin our dive into the ISPL-US data we feel it important to be transparent about the *selected findings* that we have chosen to highlight in this report. We made selection decisions based on our desire to provide a report that would (a) include voices from across a variety of functional areas (e.g., academic advising, orientation, campus activities, residence life); (b) offer practical and pragmatic guidance for those who fund, hire, train, and supervise peer leaders (PLs) on their campuses; and, again, (c) highlight a small number of contemporary issues in higher education that might be addressed (in part) through thoughtful design of PL experiences.

In Chapter 1 we provided a brief overview of the literature on the benefits of peer leadership in higher education to make the foundational argument that peer leadership is a promising high-impact practice (HIP) worth paying attention to and prioritizing on a campus, just like other HIPs formally listed by the American Association of Colleges & Universities (AAC&U) (Kuh, 2008). Here in Chapter 2, we extend this argument by reviewing the findings of recent research on peer leadership that both highlight avenues for ongoing inquiry and illuminate the connection between peer leadership and contemporary higher education concerns.

What do we Know About the Impact of Peer Leadership and What do we Still Need to Know?

As discussed in Chapter 1, peer leadership is growing in its application and importance to broader higher education efforts (Keup, 2020; van der Meer et al., 2022; Young et al., 2023). Though an extensive review of the recent research on peer leadership is beyond the scope of this chapter, we feel it helpful to highlight several key themes that have emerged in the research literature since the last administration of the ISPL and which help to frame some of the overall goals of this research report. Specifically, we have identified access, equity, and inclusion; belonging; and extended benefits of engagement as a PL as notable topics within the conversation on peer leadership as well as in higher education more broadly.

Access, Equity, and Inclusion in Peer Leadership

Despite growing evidence of the short- and long-term impact of peer leadership, we fear that these growth-promoting opportunities are not widely available to all college students. More specifically, the structural features of PL roles (e.g., compensation, training demands, hours required, requirements for past leadership) often serve as barriers for increasing numbers of students. Various aspects of students' identities—including financial status, first-generation status, ethnicity, and family or childcare responsibilities—play a significant role in determining whether students seek out or even have access to PLs (Ardoin & martinez, 2019; Houze, 2021; Womble, 2021).

While being a PL has transformative potential, these critical experiential learning opportunities are often reserved for students with the privilege of both time and relative financial stability (Young & Keup, 2018). To illustrate, in the 2023 ISPL-US, slightly more than 30% of participants reported eligibility to receive Pell Grants (a funding program based on financial need of college students) compared to 45% of respondents who signaled that they were not Pell-eligible (see Figure 2.1). Further, 24% of participants in the survey reported being first-generation compared to 76% reporting that any parent or guardian had earned a four-year degree (see Figure 2.2). Thus, for campuses working to close achievement gaps and broaden access to educative experiences on their campus, peer leadership is an area ripe with opportunity.

Peer Leadership and Belonging

Given peer leadership's promise as a potential avenue for addressing issues of access and equity in higher education, it should come as no surprise that these same sorts of experiences serve as a potent source of belonging for minoritized students (Womble, 2021). Historically, institutions have placed the onus for belonging on the shoulders of students with unhelpful platitudes—frequently shared in spaces like new student orientation and first-year seminars— such as "get involved," "find your space," or "put yourself out there." However, as Lisa Nunn (2021) has skillfully argued, belonging is something that institutions are both positioned and obligated to *offer* to students.

Peer leadership has been shown to provide those who serve as PLs with opportunities for meaningful engagement with faculty and peers that, consequently, increases their sense of belonging (van der Meer, 2022). Additionally, when students on the margins are, again, offered opportunities to serve in PL roles, they report that these experiences help them feel like they are making a meaningful contribution to their campus, are valued and needed by their institutions, and doing work that really matters (Ribera et al., 2017; Womble, 2021). While we know that engagement as a PL can be a source of belonging for minoritized students and lead to more equitable outcomes across demographic groups, questions remain about how the structure and design of these experiences may be denying access to particular segments of an increasingly diverse population of U.S. college students.

The Extended Benefits of Peer Leadership

One thing that is becoming abundantly clear is that serving as a PL does not just provide immediate or proximate benefit to students who serve in these roles. As outlined in Chapter 1, PLs report gains and growth *during* college. But the power of peer leadership extends well past graduation to impact postgraduate and employability outcomes (van der Meer et al., 2022; Young & Keup, 2018). Because peer leadership offers students an opportunity to function in an authentic work environment, it is associated with a range of graduate attributes critical for students' future success such as communication, critical thinking, collaborative ability, leadership, and ethical responsibility (Chilvers & Waghorne, 2018; Laurs, 2018; Scott et al., 2019).

Additionally, peer leadership plays a key role in helping students develop a variety of employability skills by addressing gaps in students' course curricula and fostering skills not explicitly addressed in academic coursework, including improved technical and organizational skills, increased professionalism, and a greater appreciation for workplace mentoring (Carr et al., 2018). The students who serve in PL roles are becoming increasingly likely to seek out these opportunities, not just as a source of income or way of being involved on campus, but as an essential aspect of their career or graduate school preparation (Womble, 2021; Young & Keup, 2018). However, as discussed in Chapter 1, the value of peer leadership as preparation for future endeavors depends highly on the design and structure of the experience. This includes the degree to which those who administer these programs support PLs in making meaning of their experiences and connecting this meaning to future endeavors (Wawrzynski & Lemon, 2019), offer opportunities for close engagement with faculty and staff in work that matters to the institution, and engage in intentional mentoring and modeling in their interactions with peer leaders (Bunting & Williams, 2017).

Key Conceptual Frameworks for Analyzing and Applying Findings

As outlined in this chapter, there is a growing body of research demonstrating the significant and lasting impact that being a PL can have upon college students. Consequently, the research on HIPs serves as a helpful framework for analyzing the results of the ISPL-US and considering how these data can inform efforts to further refine and strengthen the experiences provided to PLs on college campuses. As mentioned in Chapter 1, HIPs include a variety of educational practices that yield significant educational benefits for college students, particularly those from demographic groups who have historically been excluded and underserved by higher education (Kuh, 2008). AAC&U has formally identified 11 practices—primarily through research at NSSE, but often validated through other research (Brownell & Swaner, 2010; Kuh, 2008; Kuh et al., 2017)—that have demonstrated strong and beneficial outcomes for students. However, these outcomes have been contingent on the educational structure and implementation fidelity of the practices, more than simply implementing an initiative under one of these headings (Kinzie et al., 2021; Kuh et al., 2017; see also, Topping, 2005). Kuh and O'Donnell's (2013) description of the characteristics of HIPs offers a valuable framework for structuring experiences that might have this "high impact" on student outcomes, including peer leadership. Consequently, we have based our analysis and discussion of ISPL-US findings upon these eight characteristics:

- Performance expectations set at appropriately high levels;
- Significant investment of time and effort by students over an extended period;
- Interactions with faculty and peers about substantive matters;
- Experiences with people and circumstances that differ from those with which students are familiar;
- Frequent, timely, and constructive feedback;
- Periodic, structured opportunities to reflect and integrate learning;
- Opportunities to discover the relevance of learning through real-world applications; and
- Public demonstration of competence.

In addition to Kuh and O'Donnell's (2013) framework of the characteristics of HIPs, we have also drawn upon Lave and Wenger's (1991) conceptualization of *legitimate peripheral participation* to make meaning of the data gathered from ISPL-US participants. In their foundational discussion of *legitimate peripheral participation*, Lave and Wenger define learning as the process by which inexperienced or novice members of a learning community move toward fuller participation and growing expertise through participating in authentic community practices with more experienced members of the community. Due to the nature of peer leadership—specifically, the opportunities it provides peer leaders to participate alongside faculty and staff in supporting the learning of students—we wanted to draw upon a theoretical framework that acknowledges the critical role that participation and relationships play in the learning process. *Legitimate peripheral participation* was particularly apt for this task. In the analysis and discussion that follows we will highlight three modes of learning and transition—*community, participation,* and *becoming* (Young & Bunting, 2024)—that are grounded in *legitimate peripheral participation* and that serve as helpful analytical tools for considering how campuses might deepen the impact of peer leadership experiences. Across this report we will demonstrate that taking on a PL role positions students for an experience that can reshape and refine their identities. Put another way, being a PL can be an experience of identity and becoming; it has the potential to transform both students and campus communities.

Together, these two conceptual frameworks—HIPs and *legitimate peripheral participation*—helped us frame three main avenues of inquiry for this general discussion and overview of the ISPL findings:

- Who has access to meaningful peer leadership experiences?

- To what extent might participating as peer leaders provide student leaders with a pathway to belonging?

- How much do the features of PL programs in the ISPL-US align with the elements of HIPs?

Access to the Pathways Offered by Peer Leadership

As discussed previously, there are powerful benefits to the PL experience. However, these benefits only result if clear pathways to these experiences are created and sustained by campus professionals. Moreover, these paths are sometimes hidden from or even denied to some students, particularly those who have been historically underserved in higher education (Houze, 2021; Young & Keup, 2018). Ardoin and martinez (2019) have articulated this idea well:

> Student leadership and involvement roles are glorified on college campuses, yet we ignore all the factors that prevent people from getting involved… To be a student leader, one must have a degree of freedom, whether that is financial or time. (p. 41)

Who Participates as Peer Leaders in the United States?

We have approached our analysis of the ISPL-US data with these issues of access and equity in mind. We begin by examining who is currently participating as PLs in the United States. In general, PLs are academic high achievers; indeed, the average GPA of students in our sample was 3.60 (SD = .44). This makes sense as many PL positions have minimum GPA requirements, particularly those roles connected to academic programs (Young et al., 2019).

The six most common broad major areas for students in PL roles were:

- Social sciences: 20.2%

- Business, management, marketing: 14.3%

- Health professions and related programs: 12.9%

- Life sciences: 11.8%

- Humanities: 10.5%

- Education: 9.2%

Overall, the largest proportions of PLs in this sample were found in social sciences and humanities, followed by majors in helping professions. Notwithstanding, more than one quarter (26.3%) reported majoring in STEM (Science, Technology, Engineering, and Mathematics) fields such as life sciences, engineering, and physical sciences.

Table 2.1 presents the composition of respondents by gender. Consistent with previous surveys of PLs (see Heys & Wawrzynski, 2013; Lemon et al., 2021; Young et al., 2019; Young & Keup, 2019), women outnumber PLs of other genders, representing more than two thirds of this sample. An additional 3.5% of students reported their gender as nonbinary, genderqueer, or genderfluid along with 0.5% who reported being agender. This represents a greater degree of gender diversity than found in previous surveys.

Table 2.1

Gender of Peer Leaders Participating in 2023 ISPL-US (n = 1398)

	Overall	
Gender	**Freq.**	**%**
Agender	6	0.5
Man	364	26.8
Woman	956	67.8
Nonbinary/Genderqueer/Genderfluid	52	3.5
Two spirit	0	0.0
Another identity	4	0.3
Prefer not to say	16	1.0

Nearly three quarters of participants identified as White (74.7%; see Table 2.2), while the next largest group were students identifying as Hispanic, Chicano/a, Latino/a (14.8%). Black or African American students were underrepresented in the sample compared to their enrollments in higher education (6.7%, compared to national participation rates of 13%; National Center for Education Statistics, 2023). Whether this is due to racial demographics of participating institutions or represents lower participation rates in PL roles is worthy of further investigation.

Table 2.2

Race and Ethnicity of Peer Leaders Participating in 2023 ISPL-US (n = 1396)

	Overall	
Race or ethnicity	**Freq.**	**%**
American Indian or Alaska Native	11	0.8
Asian or Asian American	120	8.6
Black or African American	94	6.7
Hispanic, Chicano/a, or Latino/a	206	14.8
Native Hawaiian or other Pacific Islander	12	0.9
White	1043	74.7
Other	25	1.8
I prefer not to respond	18	1.3

Finally, we present two demographic categories commonly used as proxies for class or socioeconomic status. A little less than a third (31.1%) of peer leaders in the sample reported that they were eligible for financial aid under the Pell Grant program, a need-based grant provided by the federal government (see Figure 2.1). However, nearly a quarter of respondents (24.2%) reported not knowing whether they were eligible for a Pell Grant. Without further information, it is difficult to discern whether this represents students who are unaware of the program because of a lack of need, or unaware of the name of the aid program for other reasons such as unfamiliarity with details around financial aid. Similarly, nearly a quarter of respondents (23.7%) identified as first-generation students, or students where no parent or guardian had earned a four-year college degree (see Figure 2.2).

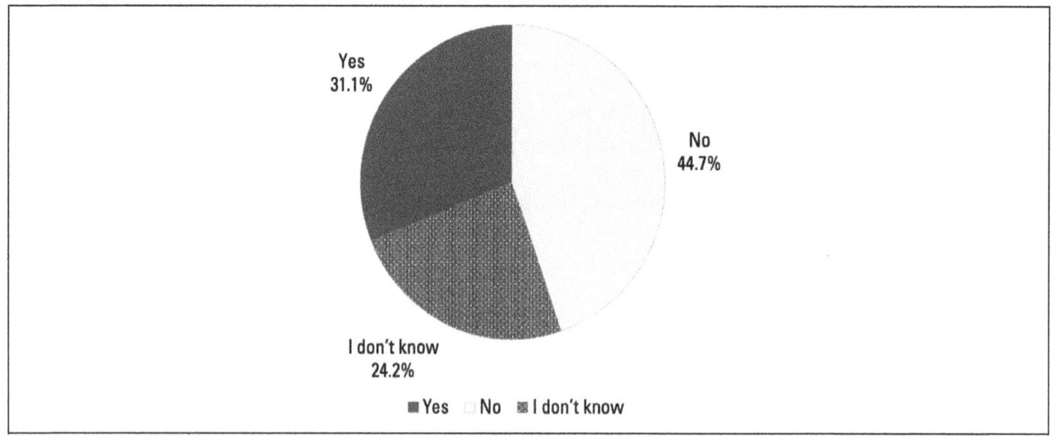

Figure 2.1. Percentage of peer leaders reporting Pell eligibility (*n* = 1395).

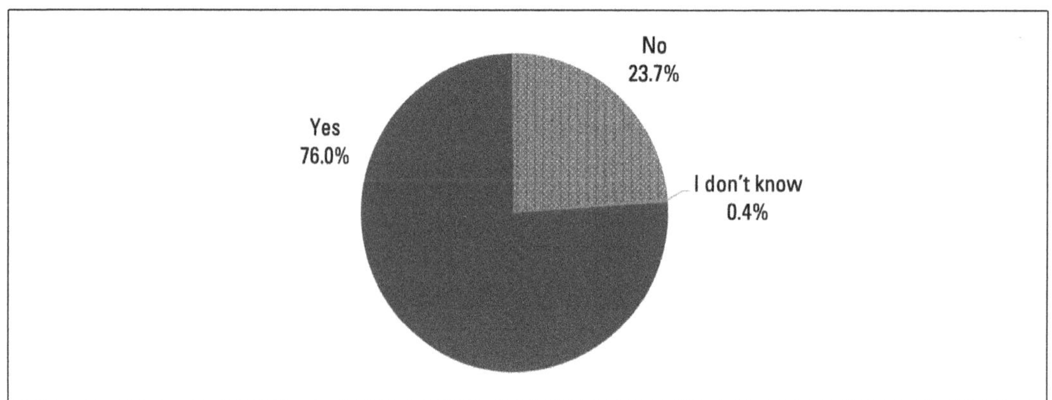

Figure 2.2. Percentage of peer leaders reporting continuing-generation status (i.e., any parent or guardian earning a four-year degree; *n* = 1395).

Understanding Motivation and Access to Peer Leader Experiences

Because access to PL experiences is contingent on students' beliefs that they have the freedom to pursue such roles, understanding their motivations for taking on peer leadership opportunities is critical. Students most frequently report taking on a PL role to help other students (88.4%), share knowledge with others (75.8%), and take on challenges and develop skills (73.2%; see Table 2.4). Financial concerns are also a motivator for many students, including desires to earn an income (62.0%), and receiving reduced tuition or housing (14.5%). Desires to become involved in the university community (60.9%), to give back to the college or university (39.4%), and to become involved in the running of the institution (18.7%), are also common. This aligns with our arguments in our writing on rethinking student transitions (see Young & Bunting, 2024) that offering students opportunities to participate in their campus community via actively leading and teaching their peers is critical to both supporting successful transitions through college, but also in supporting the personal growth, meaningful learning, and becoming institutions' promise to provide to students.

Table 2.3

Motivation of Peer Leaders to Take on PL Role (*n* = 1341)

	Overall	
Motivation	**Freq.**	**%**
Helping other students	1185	88.4
Sharing knowledge with others	1017	75.8
Personal/professional challenges and skill development	981	73.2
Earning an income while studying	832	62.0
Involvement in the University community, meet new people	816	60.9
Enjoyment or experience	802	59.8
Current or future job prospects	720	53.7
Giving back to or serving the University	528	39.4
Academic development - improve subject knowledge	431	32.1
Involvement in academic/governance aspects of the University	251	18.7
Reduced study/accommodation fees	194	14.5
Other (please specify):	29	2.2

In general, motivation for engaging in peer leadership does not vary by first-generation status or Pell eligibility, with a few notable exceptions. First, first-generation and Pell-eligible students reported involvement, connection, and contributing to the university as motivators for becoming a PL more frequently than their continuing-generation or non-Pell-eligible peers (see Tables 2.4 and 2.5). Conversely, continuing-generation students more frequently reported desiring to improve future employability than their first-generation peers (see Table 2.5). Interestingly, both Pell eligible and non-Pell eligible PLs were equally motivated by the opportunity to earn an income while in school (61.7% and 66.5%, respectively). However, students who reported not knowing whether they were Pell-eligible reported this same motivator at significantly lower rates. This finding merits further investigation but suggests that those who reported not knowing their Pell eligibility might just lack financial need and therefore know less about the program.

Table 2.4

Motivation of Peer Leaders to Take on PL Role by First-Generation Status (*n* = 1333)

	Continuing generation (*n* = 1013)	First generation (*n* = 320)	
Motivation	**%**	**%**	***p***
Helping other students	88.4	88.4	
Sharing knowledge with others	75.9	75.9	
Personal/professional challenges and skill development	72.2	75.9	
Earning an income while studying	62.8	59.7	
Involvement in the University community, meet new people	58.4	68.1	**
Enjoyment or experience	59.9	59.4	
Current or future job prospects	55.3	48.1	*
Giving back to the University	38.3	41.9	
Academic development - improve subject knowledge	32.6	30.9	
Involvement in academic/governance aspects of the University	16.8	24.7	**
Reduced study/accommodation fees	13.8	16.3	
Other	2.2	2.2	

Note. *p < .05, **p < .01

Table 2.5

Motivation of Peer Leaders to Take on PL Role by Pell Eligibility (*n* = 1333)

Motivation	Pell eligible (*n* = 418)	Not Pell eligible or "I don't know" (*n* = 920)	*p*
	%	%	
Helping other students	91.4	87.0	
Sharing knowledge with others	78.9	74.6	
Personal/professional challenges and skill development	75.6	72.2	
Earning an income while studying	61.7	62.2	***[a]
Involvement in the University community, meet new people	69.4	57.1	***
Enjoyment or experience	61.2	59.1	
Current or future job prospects	55.0	53.2	
Giving back to the University	45.2	36.7	*
Academic development - improve subject knowledge	30.9	32.7	
Involvement in academic/governance aspects of the University	23.9	16.4	**
Reduced study/accommodation fees	16.3	13.7	
Other	1.7	2.4	

Note. *p < .05, **p < .01, ***p<.001.

[a]Disaggregated percentages between "Pell Eligible" (61.7%), "Not Pell Eligible" (66.5%), and "I don't know" (54.2%) suggest the low *p*-value is due to the proportion of students who reported not knowing their Pell eligibility

Peer Leadership as a Pathway to Belonging

Peer leadership also provides a powerful pathway to a *sense of belonging* on campus. Sense of belonging concerns social support, connectedness, and feeling valued and important to the campus community (Strayhorn, 2012). Belonging happens through mutual and reciprocal relationships; there is a benefit that comes to the individual from belonging to the group and to the group that comes from the connectedness of its members (Nunn, 2021; Strayhorn, 2012). Conversely, lack of a sense of belonging "leaves individuals feeling adrift, isolated, and unanchored to the community" (Nunn, 2021, p. 9).

Belonging is not inevitable—it must be offered by the community (Nunn, 2021). Student leadership, in general, is a potent source of belonging for minoritized (Womble, 2021), lower-income, and first-generation students (Means & Pyne, 2017). This is due, in part, to the way that student leadership invites students to become active participants in the work of the institution, thereby offering forms of membership and community not available to the general student population. Indeed, as asserted at the beginning of the chapter, peer leadership positions offer students the chance to be *legitimate peripheral participants* (Lave & Wenger, 1991). Notwithstanding, pathways to belonging may be fraught and full of challenges for students from minoritized populations (Paredes-Collins & McIntosh, 2020). For instance, Students of Color frequently feel that their voice does not matter on a campus that is full of cultural signals that the environment was built with White students in mind and that there are shortages of spaces where students can express their authentic selves (Paredes-Collins & McIntosh, 2020).

Nunn (2021) described three domains of college belonging: social, academic, and campus-community belonging. We find these domains useful in describing the multiplicity of ways peer leadership experiences may be leveraged to foster belonging among PLs. In what follows, we explore how peer leadership can contribute to a sense of belonging in each of these three domains. Moreover, because sense of belonging is not consistent across student groups, we will further disaggregate by first-generation status, Pell eligibility, and race and ethnicity.

Social Belonging

From the beginnings of peer leadership on U.S. college campuses, institutions have recognized the value of PLs in facilitating social belonging (Shook & Keup, 2012). Indeed, for many PLs, (e.g., orientation leaders, resident assistants, student programming boards), fostering social belonging is an explicit expectation. This is interesting given that finding social belonging is also one of the primary reasons students seek out PL roles (see previous section on PL motivation). Therefore, PLs occupy a unique liminal space as they simultaneously offer social belonging to others while also seeking it out for themselves.

Table 2.6 provides an overview of the proportion of students who reported participating in socially-oriented PL roles. The most frequent roles included student clubs and organizations (23.7%), orientation (17.9%), and residence life (17.0%). The prevalence of these roles is consistent with previous administrations of the NSPL (Keup, 2012; Keup, 2016; Young & Keup, 2013).

Table 2.6

Socially-Oriented PL Roles (n = 1382)

Peer leader role	Overall	
	Freq.	%
Student clubs and organization(s)	328	23.7
Orientation	248	17.9
Residence hall	235	17.0
Campus activities	211	15.3
Greek life	124	9.0
Community service or service-learning	100	7.2
Religious	86	6.2
Student government	85	6.2
Athletics	62	4.5
Multicultural affairs	45	3.3
Counseling or mental health	30	2.2
Outdoor or recreational sports	24	1.7
Student productions or media	24	1.7
Outdoor orientation	19	1.4
International student office	10	0.7
Physical health	6	0.4

Overall, students reported that their engagement with peers had increased due to participation as a PL. The average response was 6.13 (SD = 0.92) on a 7-point scale, indicating that students felt strongly that being a PL contributed to greater amounts of meaningful interactions with their peers. These data support the argument that being a PL allows students to both offer and receive a sense of belonging on their campus.

Earlier, we pointed to research that suggests peer leadership is a particularly powerful source of belonging for first-generation, low-income, and racially minoritized students. In Table 2.7, we share responses to the question about increased meaningful interaction with peers disaggregated along these lines. As seen in Table 2.7, first-generation PLs reported higher levels of agreement (M = 6.22, SD = 0.86) that their experience led to greater amounts of meaningful interaction with peers than their continuing-generation counterparts (M = 6.10, SD = 0.94). A follow-up t-test found that this difference was statistically significant (t = 2.04, df = 1259; p = .041). Pell-eligible students also reported greater agreement that the PL role led to more meaningful interaction with peers ($M = 6.18$, $SD = 0.93$) compared to those who were not Pell-eligible or did not know their status. However, a follow-up ANOVA found that these differences were not statistically significant.

Finally, Asian or Asian-American ($M = 6.28$, $SD = 0.82$) and Latino/a ($M = 6.22$, $SD = 0.98$) PLs, as well as those who indicated "Other" racial or ethnic designations ($M = 6.29$, $SD = 1.01$), reported comparatively greater amounts of agreement that they increased their meaningful interactions with peers via their PL roles. Because these categories were reported as "select all that apply," it did not allow us to easily compare means using t-tests or ANOVAs but suggests the need for further research exploring how PL experiences contribute to social belonging for Asian and Latino/a students compared to students from other racial and ethnic groups.

Table 2.7

Peer Leaders' Reported Increase in Meaningful Interaction with Peers by Demographic Groups ($n = 1259$)

Peer leader role	Meaningful interactions with peers	
	M	**SD**
First-Generation Status		
Continuing Generation	248	17.9
First Generation	235	17.0
Pell Grant Eligibility	211	15.3
Pell Eligible	124	9.0
Not Pell Eligible	100	7.2
"I don't know"	86	6.2
Race or Ethnicity	85	6.2
American Indian or Alaska Native	62	4.5
Asian or Asian American	45	3.3
Black or African American	30	2.2
Hispanic, Chicano/a, or Latino/a	24	1.7
Native Hawaiian or other Pacific Islander	24	1.7
White	19	1.4
Other	6	0.4

Note. Participants were asked to rate their agreement with the statement that their meaningful interactions with peers had increased because of their peer leader experiences on a seven-point scale of agreement from "greatly decreased" (1) to "greatly increased" (7).

Academic Sense of Belonging

Nunn (2021) indicated that sense of belonging in academic spaces is an equally important facet of college belonging. Students with confidence that they belong academically engage more fully in their learning (Paredes-Collins & McIntosh, 2020; Strayhorn, 2022). PLs have been used widely in academic spaces to provide a valuable range of services to their peers to improve both their academic competence and confidence (Nunn, 2021; Skipper & Keup, 2017; Young et al., 2019). In so doing, PLs in academic roles participate and contribute to academic communities of practice (Lave & Wenger, 1991; Nunn, 2021). This is an important form of developing ownership and membership in academic spaces, which is connected to identity as a learner and sense of community in academic spaces (Schreiner et al., 2020; Young & Bunting, 2024). As a result, PLs in academic roles have been shown to develop greater levels of confidence in their own academic competence (Skipper & Keup, 2017; Young et al., 2019; Young et al., 2023), which becomes an important proxy for academic belonging which we employ in the following section.

Table 2.8 presents an overview of PL roles that support students in curricular spaces on campus. The PL roles focused on the academic aspects of campus life named most frequently include the first-year experience

(FYE; 34.5%), peer advisors (21.1%), teaching or lab assistants (19.8%), and tutors (14.7%). These results are also consistent with previous research on peer leaders (see Greenfield et al., 2013; Latino & Ashcraft, 2012; Young, 2019; Young & Hopp, 2014).

Table 2.8

Academically-Oriented PL Roles (*n* = 1382)

	Overall	
	Freq.	**%**
First-year experience	477	34.5
Academic – peer advisor	292	21.1
Academic – other (e.g., teaching assistant, lab assistant)	273	19.8
Academic – tutor	203	14.7
Academic – Supplemental Instruction leader	124	9.0
Admissions	54	3.9
Multicultural affairs	45	3.3
Study abroad	18	1.3
Judicial affairs or student conduct	7	0.5
Financial literacy	6	0.4

The ISPL-US offers several indicators about how being a PL contributes to the academic competence and confidence of PLs in academic roles. Table 2.9 presents the average responses to three questions about increased academic success as a direct result of the PL experience: (a) overall academic skills, (b) GPA, and (c) overall academic performance which, while not direct measures of belonging, contribute to students' overall academic confidence and, therefore, are proxies of students' sense that they are successful and belong to their academic communities of practice. Students reported slight agreement with each of the three indicators, with the average agreement about increased academic skills a 5.20 (*SD* = 1.20), overall academic performance a 4.52 (*SD* = 1.10), and GPA a 4.29 (*SD* = 1.10) on a 7-point scale. While this seems lukewarm compared to other outcomes in the survey and presented in this report, we suspect that a ceiling effect is at work in that these students are likely already high academic achievers and might not report higher increases because of commonly used measures of academic success that have maximums (e.g., grades, exam scores).

Table 2.9

Peer Leaders' Reported Increase in Academic Success

"To what degree have the following changed as a direct result of your peer leadership experiences?"	**M**	**SD**
Academic skills (*n* = 1275)	5.20	1.20
Your GPA (*n* = 1225)	4.29	1.06
Your overall academic performance (*n* = 1231)	4.52	1.10

Note. Participants were asked to rate the degree to which serving as a peer leader impacted their experiences across various academic outcomes on a seven-point scale of agreement from "greatly decreased" (1) to "greatly increased" (7).

When the responses to these questions are disaggregated (see Table 2.10), notable patterns emerge. First, average ratings for the contribution of peer leadership participation to increased academic success were consistently higher for first-generation students compared to their continuing-generation peers across all three measures. Follow-up *t*-tests demonstrated that there are significant differences between these average ratings for increased GPA (t = 2.32, df = 423.16, p = .021) and overall academic performance (t = 4.34, df = 430.67, p > .001). No discernible pattern in differences for students based on their Pell eligibility were identified. Pell-eligible students rated academic skills and overall academic performance comparatively higher. However, they also rated increased GPA at the same level as students who reported not being eligible for the Pell Grant. Follow-up ANOVA tests found that these differences were not statistically significant.

Patterns for academic success by race and ethnicity indicated that Indigenous students more consistently reported that peer leadership experiences contributed to their academic belonging. Conversely, White students were more consistent in reporting that peer leadership did not contribute to their academic sense of belonging. More research is warranted to disentangle the diverse ways in which participation in peer leadership does or does not contribute to academic belonging, particularly from an intersectional lens.

Table 2.10

Peer Leaders' Reported Increase in Academic Success by Demographic Groups

Demographics	Academic skills (*n* = 1275)		Increased GPA (*n* = 1225)		Overall Academic Performance (*n* = 1231)	
	M	*SD*	*M*	*SD*	*M*	*SD*
First-Generation Status						
Continuing Generation	5.19	1.16	4.25	1.00	4.44	1.04
First Generation	5.27	1.31	4.45	1.23	4.77	1.24
Pell Grant Eligibility						
Pell Eligible	5.30	1.25	4.28	1.08	4.62	1.14
Not Pell Eligible	5.16	1.19	4.29	1.04	4.44	1.07
"I don't know"	5.17	1.14	4.36	1.09	4.56	1.10
Race or Ethnicity						
American Indian or Alaska Native	5.44	1.13	5.11	0.93	5.33	1.32
Asian or Asian American	5.36	1.12	4.38	0.96	4.62	1.05
Black or African American	5.12	1.27	4.40	1.32	4.74	1.17
Hispanic, Chicano/a, or Latino/a	5.45	1.26	4.48	1.21	4.79	1.25
Native Hawaiian or other Pacific Islander	5.13	1.64	4.01	0.89	4.38	1.51
White	5.17	1.18	4.25	1.02	4.45	1.06
Other	5.79	1.18	4.68	0.95	4.95	1.31

Note. Participants were asked to rate the degree to which serving as a peer leader impacted their experiences across various academic outcomes on a seven-point scale of agreement from "greatly decreased" (1) to "greatly increased" (7).

Campus-Community Sense of Belonging

While social and academic belonging are important indicators of overall sense of belonging, they have been shown to be distinct—and distinctly important—from the sense of belonging to the overall campus community (Nunn, 2021). Students may feel comfortable and find membership in social pockets across campus or they might find spaces where they feel that they fit in and are welcomed in academic spaces. But campus-community belonging is a measure of whether students feel an overall membership and acceptance in the broader institution (Nunn, 2021).

Peer leadership can provide an opportunity for students to feel like they not only belong in social and academic spaces, but also to the overall work of the institution, which, as we shared earlier, is a particularly important motivator for first-generation and Pell-eligible students. Table 2.11 presents indicators of peer leaders' overall sense of belonging to the campus community: (a) feeling they belong and are welcome at the institution, (b) student's desire to stay at the institution and graduate, and (c) feeling that the student is contributing to the campus community. Students reported general agreement with each of the three indicators, with the average agreement about increased feeling of being welcome and belonging a 5.86 (SD = 1.17), desire to stay and graduate a 5.62 (SD = 1.30) and feeling that they are contributing to the campus community a 6.16 (SD = 0.96) on a 7-point scale.

Table 2.11

Peer Leaders' Reported Increase in Campus-Community Sense of Belonging

"To what degree have the following college or university experiences changed as a direct result of your peer leadership experiences?"	*M*	*SD*
Your feeling that you belong and are welcome at your institution (n = 1269)	5.86	1.17
Your desire to stay at your institution and graduate (n = 1268)	5.62	1.30
Your feeling that you are contributing to your campus community (n = 1254)	6.16	0.96

Note. articipants were asked to rate the degree to which serving as a peer leader impacted their experiences across various campus-community belonging outcomes on a seven-point scale of agreement from "greatly decreased" (1) to "greatly increased" (7).

As stated previously, data from the ISPL-US provide evidence that peer leadership is an especially important pathway to a strong sense of belonging for first-generation, Pell-eligible, and racially minoritized students. Table 2.12 presents the responses to indicators of campus-community belonging, broken down by these demographic groupings. First, average ratings for the contribution of peer leadership participation to increased campus-community belonging were consistently higher for first-generation students as compared to their continuing-generation peers across all three measures. Follow-up t-tests demonstrate that there are significant differences between these average ratings for feeling of belonging at the institution (t = 2.47, df = 1261, p = .013), desire to stay at institution and graduate (t = 2.32, df = 512.67, p < .001), and feelings of contributing to campus community (t = 2.182, df = 1272, p = .029). Pell eligible PLs also consistently reported that these indicators of belonging were increased by participation in their roles at higher rates than those who were not eligible or those who reported not knowing their eligibility. Follow-up ANOVA tests found that Pell-eligible students reported their desire to stay at the institution and graduate increased because of participation as a PL at higher rates than those did not (F = 9.70, df = 1265, p < .001). Response patterns for feelings of belonging by race and ethnicity indicated that Latino/a students more consistently reported that their peer leadership experiences contributed to their overall sense of campus-community belonging. Interestingly, peer leadership as a way for students to feel that they were contributing to the campus community appear to be stronger indicators of belonging for Asian, African American, Latino/a, Native Hawaiian or Pacific Islander, and White students, as their average rating for this indicator was higher than the other two. More research is warranted to understand the variety of ways in which participation in peer leadership provides pathways to belonging with the overall campus community, particularly from an intersectional lens.

Table 2.12

Peer Leaders' Reported Increase in Campus-Community Sense of Belonging by Demographic Groups

Demographics	Feeling of belonging at institution (*n* = 1269)		Desire to stay at institution and graduate (*n* = 1268)		Feeling of contributing to campus community (*n* = 1254)	
	M	*SD*	*M*	*SD*	*M*	*SD*
First-Generation Status						
Continuing Generation	5.81	1.17	5.53	1.29	6.13	0.96
First Generation	6.03	1.12	5.92	1.26	6.28	0.92
Pell Grant Eligibility						
Pell Eligible	5.96	1.15	5.85	1.28	6.23	0.91
Not Pell Eligible	5.80	1.17	5.51	1.31	6.13	0.96
"I don't know"	5.86	1.15	5.55	1.24	6.13	0.98
Race or Ethnicity						
American Indian or Alaska Native	5.78	1.20	5.67	1.41	5.67	1.23
Asian or Asian American	5.97	1.07	5.62	1.30	6.15	0.96
Black or African American	5.85	1.21	5.70	1.42	6.21	0.90
Hispanic, Chicano/a, or Latino/a	6.08	1.13	6.02	1.23	6.32	0.92
Native Hawaiian or other Pacific Islander	5.60	1.71	5.00	1.76	6.10	1.20
White	5.82	1.16	5.56	1.29	6.29	0.94
Other	6.05	1.17	5.77	1.45	6.41	0.85

Note. Participants were asked to rate the degree to which serving as a peer leader impacted their experiences across various campus-community belonging outcomes on a seven-point scale of agreement from "greatly decreased" (1) to "greatly increased" (7).

In sum, peer leadership fosters a sense of belonging by leveraging the modes of transition (Young & Bunting, 2024) referenced at the beginning of the chapter—*community, participation,* and *becoming*—by providing opportunities to actively participate in and contribute to the educational process. And when students are invited to join faculty and staff in this work, they cannot help but feel like they belong and are valued members of the campus community.

Peer Leadership as a High-Impact Practice

One of the questions raised in the Introduction to the book was whether peer leadership might be considered a HIP in its own right. To help answer this question, we designed the 2023 ISPL to provide insight into how well the experiences of survey respondents aligned with the characteristics of HIPs outlined earlier in this chapter, particularly the following five characteristics identified by Kuh and O'Donnell (2013):

- Investment of time and effort by students over an extended period,
- Interactions with faculty,
- Periodic, structured opportunities to reflect and integrate learning,
- Frequent, timely and constructive feedback, and
- Experiences with people and circumstances that differ from those with which students are familiar.

An examination of these characteristics of the PL experience allowed us to act on the invitation of Kinzie et al. (2021) to focus on the quality of implementation of peer leadership and fidelity to Kuh and O'Donnell's framework.

Investment of Time and Effort

As with any educational practice, the impact of peer leadership on students' learning and development is based, in part, on their engagement and investment in their role. To help us make this determination for students in our sample, we analyzed (a) the amount of time PLs reported spending on their particular responsibilities and duties and (b) the degree to which they were engaged in both initial and ongoing training to prepare and support them in their roles.

In general, PLs spend a significant amount of time engaged in peer leadership activities each week. In fact, most of the students in our sample (81.2%) reported spending more than five hours each week working as a PL (see Table 2.13). More research is warranted to more fully understand why a substantial number of participants (11.7%) reported spending more than 20 hours per week engaging in a PL role and whether there is a point of diminishing returns (Young et al., 2023).

Table 2.13

Average Hours per Week Spent in Peer Leader Activities in 2023 ISPL-US (n = 1354)

# of hours	Freq.	%
5 hours or less	254	18.8
6 – 10 hours	375	27.7
11 – 15 hours	272	20.1
16 – 20 hours	295	21.8
21 – 25 hours	94	6.9
26 – 30 hours	42	3.1
31 – 35 hours	9	0.7
36 – 40 hours	8	0.6
More than 40 hours	5	0.4

Respondents' reports on their engagement in training activities provide additional insight into whether PLs truly invest significant time and energy in their work. Not surprisingly, most students (87.2%) reported that they received initial training for most or all their PL roles (see Figure 2.3). Similarly, nearly three quarters of the participants in the survey (73.7%) reported that they had received ongoing formal training (see Figure 2.4).

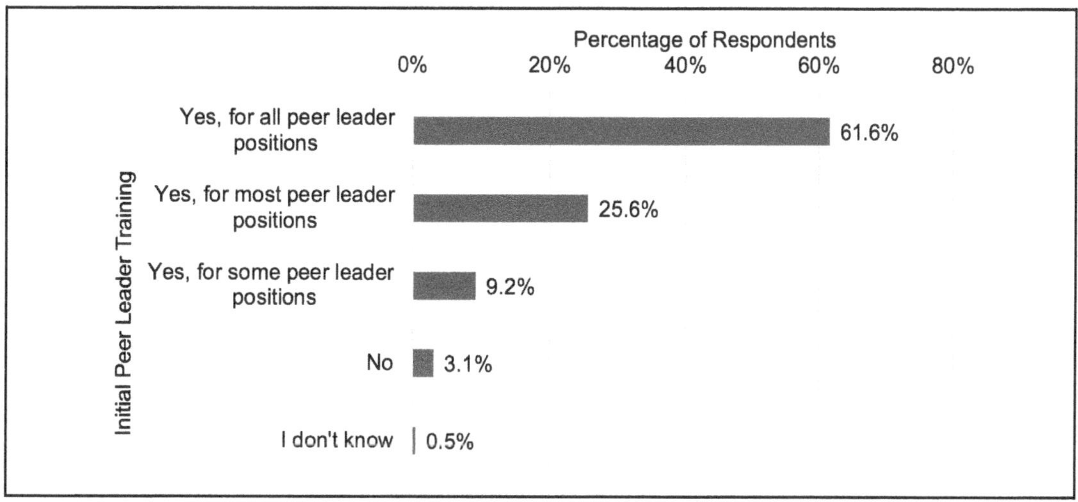

Figure 2.3. Percentage of peer leaders reporting initial training (*n* = 1340).

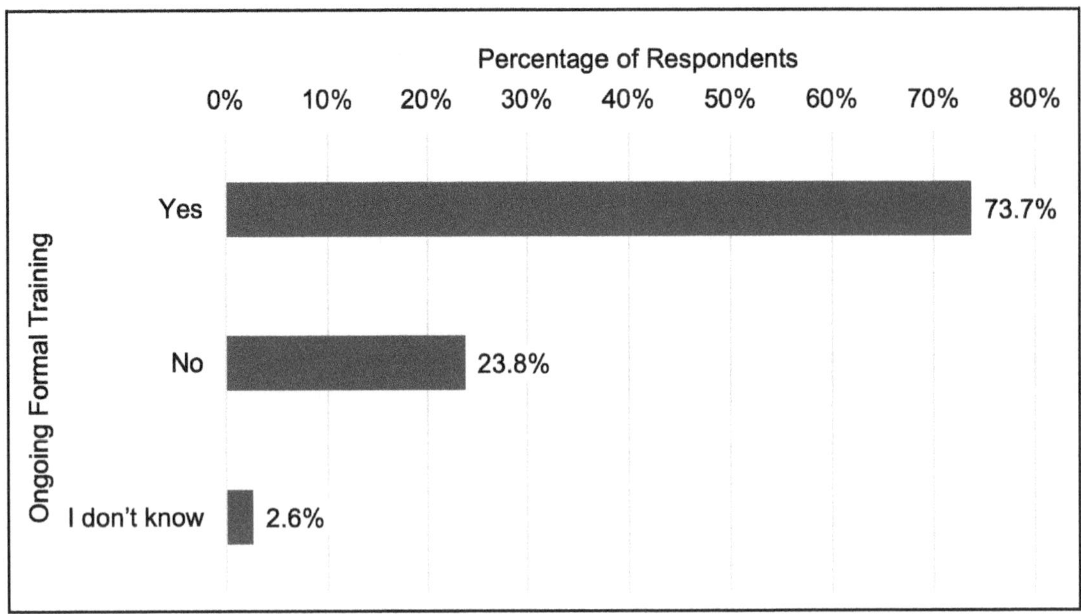

Figure 2.4. Percentage of peer leaders reporting ongoing training (*n* = 1287).

This high degree of involvement positions PLs for meaningful growth in their roles; however, as we have argued previously, the real impact of the experience is determined by how this time is spent and whether it is devoted toward practices that align with other characteristics of HIPs. Consequently, we now turn to the qualitative components of the PL experience and how the time they invest in these activities aligns with additional characteristics of HIPs.

Interactions with Faculty

The degree to which institutions provide PLs with opportunities for meaningful interactions with faculty members is one of the key criteria for evaluating whether the time invested in peer leadership is truly "high impact." Additionally, when PLs have opportunities to participate alongside faculty members and contribute to legitimate academic activities (co-teaching, providing academic advisement, supporting struggling students) they step into a powerful educative space. In these enhanced peer leadership roles, students are no longer relegated to the sidelines where they become cheap labor for mundane administrative tasks. Instead, they become co-partners, co-teachers, or apprentices through shared engagement and accountability in the core work of the institution: facilitating learning.

Additionally, research on student success has suggested that meaningful relationships with faculty members are one of the most powerful ways of enhancing student learning, student success, and even post college outcomes (e.g., Felten et al., 2016; Mayhew et al., 2016; Schreiner et al., 2020). Consequently, we were particularly interested in examining ISPL-US data to evaluate the extent to which peer leadership experiences provide PLs with high-quality interactions with faculty members.

Among ISPL-US respondents, 56% reported that their peer leadership experiences had "increased" or "greatly increased" their meaningful interactions with faculty. On the one hand, these results are encouraging: over half of the PLs in our sample have been able to connect with faculty members in significant ways. However, we also see significant room for improvement and growth in this area. We encourage practitioners to continue to explore ways in which PLs can have closer proximity to faculty members to offer increased opportunities for the sort of meaningful interactions that lead to significant learning for students. As we will discuss in the next section, these interactions are frequently vehicles for deepening the learning and growth that peer leaders experience via additional characteristics of HIPs.

Structured Opportunities for Reflection, Integration, and Feedback on Performance

An additional marker of a high-impact PL experience is the frequency with which PLs reflect on and integrate the learning they are experiencing in their role. It was encouraging, then, to find that 73.2% of the PLs in our sample reported that they had periodic opportunities to "reflect on, articulate, or integrate the learning [they] were experiencing as a peer leader." Most frequently, these opportunities came via conversations with faculty or staff supervisors (77.5% of respondents) or in group discussions that were part of training meetings with other PLs (73.1%). Table 2.14 details overall responses to this survey item.

Table 2.14

What Type of Opportunities for Reflection Were you Provided? (*n* = 967)

Mode of Reflection	**Freq.**	**%**
Regular conversations with supervising faculty/staff	749	77.5
Group discussions during training meetings	707	73.1
Written reflections (e.g., journals, weekly reports)	440	45.5
Regular conversations with a senior PL	430	44.5
Portfolio containing artifacts and reflections on learning	84	8.7

While reflection is a consistent element of peer leadership experiences, we do want to point out that much of this reflection takes place in conversations. Certainly, there is value in all forms of reflection, including oral reflection. However, these data highlight something of a missed opportunity related to engaging peer leaders in a broader range of reflective modalities, particularly written reflection. Kuh (2008) identified writing intensive experiences as HIPs, suggesting that the impact of serving as a PL could improve through thoughtful incorporation of more frequent reflective writing activities. Similarly, Kuh (2008) identified the use of e-portfolios as a HIP, yet PLs in this sample reported only rarely engaging in this type of reflection (8.7%). We call upon practitioners and researchers alike to consider how written reflection, particularly as part of a broader process of compiling a peer leadership portfolio, could further enhance the learning and growth experienced by PLs.

Nearly three quarters (74.7%) of PLs indicated that they had regular opportunities to receive feedback on their performance. And, just as interactions with supervising faculty or staff were the most common means by which PLs were engaged in reflection, meetings with faculty and staff were the most frequently cited means of receiving feedback (see Table 2.15).

Table 2.15

How was Feedback on your Performance Provided? (*n* = 991)

Feedback mechanism	**Freq.**	**%**
Meetings with a faculty or staff member	761	76.8
Surveys, questionnaires, or evaluations submitted by students	457	46.1
Meetings with a senior PL	359	36.2
As part of roleplays, simulations, or mock teaching/advising sessions	246	24.8

At this point, we want to pause to highlight the compelling evidence in support of models of peer leadership that prioritize and foster meaningful relationships with faculty members. Based on the analysis of the data we have shared in this chapter, we assert that faculty members can play a key role in peer leadership experiences. (See Chapter 9 for more recommendations.) More than simply serving as sources of supervision or guidance in performing PL tasks, these relationships are critical mechanisms for conversations and interactions that qualify peer leadership as a HIP. When institutions prioritize these interactions and design peer leadership experiences and programs that are *relationship rich* (Felten & Lambert, 2020), PLs will not only be more successful in their role, but are more likely to experience the long-lasting, transformative growth associated with traditional HIPs.

Experiences with People and Circumstances That Differ From Those With Which Students are Familiar

Not only did results of the ISPL-US provide evidence that peer leadership experiences are associated with meaningful interactions with peers, PLs also report that these interactions are the source of valuable opportunities to engage with people and backgrounds different than their own. Peer leaders reported that their experiences increased the *frequency* with which they interacted with people whose backgrounds were different than their own, as well as both their *knowledge* and *understanding* of others with differing backgrounds (see Table 2.16).

Table 2.16

Diversity Outcomes for Students Participating in Peer Leader Roles

Outcome	M	SD
Knowledge about people with backgrounds different from own	6.00	1.02
Interaction with people with backgrounds different from own	6.04	1.00
Understanding of people with backgrounds different from own	6.00	0.99

Note. Participants were asked to rate the degree to which serving as a peer leader impacted their experiences across various diversity outcomes on a seven-point scale of agreement from "greatly decreased" (1) to "greatly increased" (7).

Thus, peer leadership not only offers powerful pathways for belonging—particularly for historically marginalized students, such as first-generation and low-income students, but being a PL also facilitates students' engagement and interaction with a wider variety of people than they might otherwise through their typical experiences. Consequently, we encourage institutional leaders to consider pathways to access well-designed peer leadership programs (i.e., those that align with the characteristics of HIPs) for a wider array of marginalized and minoritized students. Improving access to these promising and high-impact experiences could be part of a broader effort to address issues of equity and inclusion by offering students opportunities for membership and contribution in a broader range of communities where they can find expanded opportunities for belonging.

Conclusion

As we conclude, we want to return to Lave and Wenger's (1991) conceptualization of *legitimate peripheral participation* and the three modes of transition that we introduced early in this chapter—*community, participation,* and *becoming.* Through this conceptual lens, learning is a sociocultural process by which novice, or inexperienced members, of a learning community gradually move toward greater levels of skill, understanding, membership, and contribution. Lave and Wenger's fundamental argument is that learning occurs as novices participate in meaningful community practices with peers and more knowledgeable, skilled, and experienced members of the community.

We see a strong parallel here to peer leadership. As we have demonstrated in this chapter, peer leadership can help students develop deeper expertise, skill, and membership in their campus community because of the way in which it both facilitates their participation in the legitimate practices of the community and brings them into relationship with "experts" such as faculty and academic advisors. Moreover, we want to highlight the finding that PLs occupy a liminal space wherein they offer a sense of belonging to others while seeking it for themselves, a condition akin to what is described in *legitimate peripheral participation.* Peer leaders play a role as intermediate experts as they engage with both novices and more experienced members of the community. This location in the community of practice enhances progressive and authentic participation of the students and fosters the kind of becoming that shapes students' sense of selves as knowers and doers. Further, when institutional leaders intentionally structure these experiences in alignment with the characteristics of HIPs (e.g., feedback, reflection, meaningful experiences with faculty), we can rightly assert that peer leadership has what it takes to be a HIP. Most importantly, when made accessible to all students—especially those historically on the margins—peer leadership can play an essential role in democratizing the transformative learning, belonging, and becoming at the heart of HIPs.

References

Ardoin, S., & martinez, b. (2019). *Straddling class in the academy: 26 stories of students, administrators, and faculty from poor and working-class backgrounds and their compelling lessons for higher education policy and practice.* Taylor & Francis. https://doi.org.10.4324/9781003447108

Brownell, J. E., & Swaner, L. E. (2010). *Five high-impact practices: Research on learning outcomes, completion, and quality.* Association of American Colleges and Universities.

Bunting, B., & Williams, D. (2017). Stories of transformation: Using personal narrative to explore transformative experience among undergraduate peer mentors. *Mentoring & Tutoring: Partnership in Learning, 25*(2), 166-184. https://doi.org/10.1080/13611267.2017.1327691

Carr, R. A., Evans-Locke, K., Abu-Saif, H., Boucher, R., & Douglas, K. (2018). Peer-learning to employable: Learnings from an evaluation of PASS attendee and facilitator perceptions of employability at Western Sydney University. *Journal of Peer Learning, 11*(1), 41-64. https://ro.uow.edu.au/ajpl/vol11/iss1/4

Chilvers, L., & Waghorne, J. (2018). Exploring PASS leadership beyond graduation. *Journal of Peer Learning, 11*(2), 5-26. http://ro.uw.edu.au/ajpl/vol11/iss1/2

Felten, P., Gardner, J. N., Schroeder, C. C., Lambert, L. M., Barefoot, B. O., & Hrabowski, F. A. (2016). *The undergraduate experience: Focusing institutions on what matters most.* John Wiley & Sons.

Felten, P., & Lambert, L. M. (2020). *Relationship-rich education: How human connections drive success in college.* Johns Hopkins University Press.

Heys, K. H., & Wawrzynski, M. R. (2013). Male peer educators: Effects of participation as peer educators on college men. *Journal of Student Affairs Research and Practice, 50*(2), 189-207. http://dx.doi.org/10.1515/jsarp-2013-0014

Houze, S. K. (2021). Social class barriers to traditional student leader roles. *New Directions for Student Leadership, 2021*(169), 77-84. https://doi.org/10.1002/yd.20423

Keup, J. R. (Ed.). (2012). *Peer leadership in higher education. New directions for higher education.* (No. 157). Jossey-Bass.

Keup, J. R. (2016). Peer leadership as an emerging high-impact practice: An exploratory study of the American experience. *Journal of Student Affairs in Africa, 4*(1): 33–52. https://doi.org/10.14426/jsaa.v4i1.143.

Keup, J. R. (2020). Peer leadership, higher education. In P. N. Teixeira & J. C. Shin (Eds.), *The international encyclopedia of higher education systems and institutions* (pp. 2202-2210). Springer Nature. https://doi.org/10.1007/978-94-017-8905-9

Kinzie, J., Silberstein, S., McCormick, A. C., Gonyea, R. M., & Dugan, B. (2021). Centering racially minoritized student voices in high-impact practices. *Change: The Magazine of Higher Learning, 53*(4), 6-14. https://doi.org/10.1080/00091383.2021.1930976

Kuh, G. D. (2008). *High-impact educational practices: What they are, who has access to them, and why they matter.* American Association of Colleges and Universities.

Kuh, G. D., & O'Donnell, K. (2013). *Ensuring quality and taking high-impact practices to scale.* American Association of Colleges and Universities.

Kuh, G. D., O'Donnell, K. & Schneider, C. G. (2017). HIPs at ten. *Change: The Magazine of Higher Learning, 49*(5), 8-16. https://doi.org/10.1080/00091383.2017.1366805

Laurs, D. E. (2018). Perceived impact of PASS leadership experience on student leaders' transferable skills development. *Journal of Peer Learning, 11*(3), 27-40. https://ro.uow.edu.au/ajpl/vol11/iss1/3

Lave, J., & Wenger, E. (1991). *Situated learning: Legitimate peripheral participation.* Cambridge University Press. https://psycnet.apa.org/doi/10.1017/CBO9780511815355

Lemon, J. D., Wawrzynski, M. R., Stefanese, A., Lechman, K., & Fouani, N. (2021). *National peer educator study national report 2020-21.* Health, Safety and Well-being Initiatives of NASPA. https://www. naspa. org/files/dmfile/NPES-National-Report-2020-21_2. pdf

Mayhew, M. J., Rockenbach, A. N., Bowman, N. A., Seifert, T. A., & Wolniak, G. C. (2016). *How college affects students: 21st century evidence that higher education works* (Vol. 3). Jossey-Bass.

Means, D.R., & Pyne, K.B. (2017). Finding my way: Perceptions of institutional support and belonging in low-income, first-generation, first-year college students. *Journal of College Student Development 58*(6), 907-924. https://dx.doi.org/10.1353/csd.2017.0071

National Center for Education Statistics (2023, August). *Characteristics of postsecondary students.* Condition of Education. https://nces.ed.gov/programs/coe/indicator/csb/postsecondary-students

Nunn, L. M. (2021). *College belonging: How first-year and first-generation students navigate campus life.* Rutgers University Press.

Paredes-Collins, K., & McIntosh, E. J. (2020). Thriving and students of color: Daily transitions on predominantly white campuses. In L. A. Schreiner, M. C. Louis, & D. D. Nelson (Eds.), *Thriving in transitions: A research-based approach to college student success* (2nd ed., pp. 79-96). University of South Carolina, National Resource Center for The First-Year Experience and Students in Transition.

Ribera, A. K., Miller, A. L., & Dumford, A. D. (2017). Sense of peer belonging and institutional acceptance in the first year: The role of high-impact practices. *Journal of College Student Development, 58*(4), 545–563. https://doi.org/10.1353/csd.2017.0042

Schreiner, L. A., Louis, M. C., & Nelson, D. D. (Eds.). (2020). *Thriving in transitions: A research-based approach to college student success* (2nd ed.). University of South Carolina, National Resource Center for The First-Year Experience and Students in Transition.

Scott, C. A., McLean, A., & Golding, C. (2019). How peer mentoring fosters graduate attributes. *Journal of Peer Learning, 12*(3), 29-44. https://ro.uow.edu.au/ajpl/vol12/iss1/3

Shook, J. L., & Keup, J. R. (2012). The benefits of peer leader programs: An overview from the literature. In J. R. Keup (Ed.), *New directions in higher education: Peer leadership in higher education* (no. 157, pp. 5-16). Jossey-Bass. https://doi.org/10.1002/he.20002

Skipper, T. L., & Keup, J. R. (2017). The perceived impact of peer leadership experiences on college academic performance. *Journal of Student Affairs Research and Practice, 54*(1), 95-108. https://doi.org/10.1080/19496591.2016.1204309

Strayhorn, T. L. (2012). Exploring the impact of Facebook and Myspace use on first-year students' sense of belonging and persistence decisions. *Journal of College Student Development, 53*(6), 783-796. https://dx.doi.org/10.1353/csd.2012.0078.

Strayhorn, T. L. (2022). Unraveling the relationship among engagement, involvement, and sense of belonging. In E. M. Bentrim and G. W. Henning (Eds.), The impact of a sense of belonging in college: Implications for student persistence, retention, and success (pp. 21-34). Stylus.

Topping, K. J. (2005). Trends in peer learning. *Educational Psychology, 25*(6), 631-645. https://doi.org/10.1080/01443410500345172

van der Meer, J., Skalicky, J., Speed, H., & Young, D. G. (2022). Focusing on the development of the whole student: An international comparative study of the perceived benefits of peer leadership in higher education. *Open Journal of Social Sciences, 10*(3), 14-35. https://doi.org/10.4236/jss.2022.103002

Wawrzynski, M. R., & Lemon, J. D. (2019). Understanding student learning outcomes of peer educators. *New Directions for Higher Education, 2019*(188), 61-69. https://doi.org/10.1002/he.20346

Womble, A. A. (2021). *"Everything I did was black. That's what I was there for": A critical grounded theory of the development of student leaders with historically marginalized identities* (Publication No. 28544232) [Doctoral dissertation, The University of Arizona]. ProQuest Dissertations & Theses Global. https://www.proquest.com/dissertations-theses/everything-i-did-was-black-that-s-what-there/docview/2554981211/se-2

Young, D. G., & Bunting, B. D. (2024). What if we rethought the ways we describe college student transitions? *About Campus.* http://dx.doi.org/10.1177/10864822241252158

Young, D. G., and Keup, J. R. (2013). *2013 National survey of peer leaders* [Data set]. University of South Carolina, National Resource Center for The First-Year Experience and Students in Transition.

Young, D. G. & Keup, J. R. (2018). To pay or not to pay: The influence of compensation as an external reward on learning outcomes of peer leaders. *Journal of College Student Development, 59*(2), 159-176. https://doi.org/10.1353/csd.2018.0015

Young, D. G., Hoffman, D. E., & Frakes Reinhardt, S. (2019). An exploration of the connection between participation in academic peer leadership experiences and academic success. *Journal of Peer Learning, 12*(1), 45-60. https://ro.uow.edu.au/ajpl/vol12/iss1/4

Young, D. G., Zeng, W., Skalicky, J., & van der Meer, J. (2023). The quality and quantity of participation in peer leader experiences and student outcomes: A cross-national validation of constructs and predictive model. *Research in Higher Education,* 1-21. https://doi.org/10.1007/s11162-023-09765-4

Part 2

Evidence of the (High) Impact of Peer Leadership: Key Functional Areas in Higher Education

Chapter 3

Peer Leadership in Orientation

Kathleen Murray
Towson University

Joe Thomas
University of Colorado Boulder

New student orientation has long been considered a best practice for integrating new students into the college environment (Council for the Advancement of Standards [CAS], 2023; Greenfield et al., 2013; Upcraft et al., 2005). It serves as a starting point for the first-year experience (FYE) and, depending on the survey, between 75% and 97% of institutions offer some sort of orientation program (Greenfield et al, 2013; NODA, 2017; Young, 2019).

While orientation programs are designed to help students with both academic and social integration to campus, academic integration is typically the primary goal of orientation programming. However, social integration, including time spent with other incoming students and peer leaders (PLs), was found to be critical in the student transition (Mann et al., 2010). Indeed, as the focus of orientation programming expanded in the 1980s, the role of the orientation student leader emerged (Mack, 2010). Orientation leaders offer an incredible service to an institution by supporting the successful transition of new students. Consequently, educators and practitioners have a duty to avoid exploiting these students by working to intentionally develop orientation leaders' skills and providing an experience that contributes to their broader success at the institution. Serving as a PL, including as an orientation leader, should not simply be approached as a student job. It is an educational experience that, if approached strategically and in alignment with clear educational outcomes, can yield impressive results.

In this chapter we will provide context and history on the emergence and evolution of the orientation leader role, discuss various orientation leader models, examine recruitment and hiring practices, and then use data from the 2023 International Survey of Peer Leaders administered in the US (ISPL-US) to provide understanding of the outcomes and impacts on the students who serve in orientation-related PL roles. Our analysis and discussion of these data will focus on the degree to which serving as an orientation leader might be considered to be a high-impact practice (HIP), as well as how orientation leader experiences impact leaders' sense of belonging. Finally, we will utilize the CAS in Higher Education (2023) as a framework for recommendations related to structuring the orientation leader role in ways that contribute to meaningful learning for those who serve in these roles.

History and Context of the Orientation Leader Role

Peer leadership roles vary in orientation programs depending upon the type of orientation program offered. Orientation leaders are "part resource, part role model, part university trivia expert, part confidante, part presenter, part facilitator" (Payne & Sedotti, 2014, p. 80). The way an institution designs the orientation leader role is often determined by the type of orientation program administered on a campus. The four most common types of orientation programming include (a) the traditional and overnight orientation or pre-enrollment program, (b) the welcome week program, (c) the first-year course program (Rode & Wolfman, 2014), and (d) virtual orientation models, which are becoming increasingly common. Responsibilities of leaders within these programs include leading small groups of incoming students, serving on panels, assisting students with course registration, planning, and supporting program administration (e.g., assisting with orientation check-in), and helping with family programming. Additionally, orientation leaders help teach traditions like the fight song or alma mater, facilitate team builders and icebreakers, lead small group discussions, and support logistical elements of the program.

A growing trend in orientation is to involve orientation leaders in supporting online or virtual orientation. The COVID-19 pandemic forced many, if not all, institutions to incorporate a virtual orientation experience into their FYE. Because of the value orientation leaders play in the transition of new students, these roles were redesigned to function in a virtual space. Like orientation leaders in face-to-face settings, virtual orientation leaders facilitate small groups, teach traditions, assist with course registration, and take attendance, all while adapting to new online environments. The virtual orientation leader role helped bring students together in what, otherwise, could have been a primarily transactional program. Table 3.1 summarizes the four primary orientation leader positions, the length of their role, and the typical hiring period.

Table 3.1

Primary Orientation Leader Positions, Duration, and Hiring Period

Orientation type	Typical duration of role	Timing of hiring
Traditional/Overnight orientation	1- or 2-day programs across the summer	Late fall or spring prior to summer
Extended orientation	Up to a week	Spring
Welcome week	Week before classes begin	Spring
Virtual orientation	Across summer	Spring

Recruiting and Hiring Orientation Leaders

Over half of the respondents (52.9%) to the ISPL-US who had served in an orientation role indicated that they applied and were interviewed for the position of orientation leader. Virtually all other respondents (41.7%) reported that they volunteered for the position and were subsequently appointed. (Note: Implications and key considerations related to volunteer orientation leader work are discussed later in the chapter.)

The timing for recruiting and hiring orientation leaders varies based on the type of orientation program implemented. Providing access to the orientation leader position begins with strong recruitment processes (Bristow, 2014). Institutions must cast a wide net to recruit a team that is reflective of the overall student population. Traditional recruitment includes posters, print and virtual materials in key campus locations such as the residence halls, dining halls, and parking garages, and conducting information sessions for students to learn more about the position. Other recruitment methods include social media campaigns, peer-to-peer referrals, and outreach to faculty and staff to nominate students. Ideally, institutions will develop recruitment strategies that allow them to target segments of the student population who might normally be underrepresented in PL roles.

Even though the timing for recruitment differs, the application and hiring process tends to be similar on most campuses. Because orientation leaders work closely with incoming students and often facilitate small groups and discussion with minimal staff support, hiring processes should include opportunities for potential orientation leaders to demonstrate the skills necessary to interact with students from a variety of backgrounds and to work autonomously in alignment with program goals.

The most typical hiring process includes a formal application, followed by both a group and individual interview (Bristow, 2014). This multi-modal process gives orientation staff more comprehensive information about candidates and facilitates a stronger selection process. Depending on the volume of applicants, some institutions review applications and only invite qualified candidates for the group portion of the process. Some institutions continue to reduce the number of applicants by only inviting selected candidates for an individual interview after observing the student in a group interview setting.

A group interview process typically includes a range of activities that encourage applicants to work together to solve a problem or to clearly communicate important information with one another, all skills orientation leaders would draw upon in small group orientation sessions. Overall, the goal of the group interview process is to understand how applicants interact with their peers, how they navigate challenging situations under pressure (e.g., while being timed or observed), and their comfort in being in front of small and large groups of new students, families, and peers (Bristow, 2014). Returning student leaders and campus partners are often invited to observe the interview process and participate in evaluating applicants.

Though rigorous, the recruitment and hiring processes of orientation leaders described above embeds several key characteristics of HIPs including, *setting performance expectations at an appropriately high level* through an application and interview process; *providing frequent, timely, and constructive feedback* through rubrics and standardized assessments of candidates; and abundant opportunities for students to *reflect on and integrate their learning* by responding to interview questions and tasks (Kuh & O'Donnell, 2013).

During the recruitment and selection phase, professionals should clearly communicate any minimum qualifications or requirements (Bristow, 2014). For example, many institutions have a minimum GPA requirement for orientation leader applicants. We encourage institutions to think carefully about these requirements. On one hand, orientation leaders are role models for incoming students, and a GPA can serve as one indicator that the prospective orientation leader has been academically successful on campus and can mentor new students on how to be academically successful. Alternatively, GPA requirements can also inadvertently serve as barriers to participation for some students. Of the students responding to the ISPL-US, 82.6% self-reported a GPA of 3.0 to 4.0.

Additional requirements may include being enrolled in a particular major (e.g., in cases where particular academic backgrounds need to be represented on the orientation team); a commitment to be enrolled (or even to abstain from enrolling) in summer courses during orientation season; a commitment to remain in the role through to the conclusion of orientation season; and availability to participate in required training or any other required workdays.

Training and Development of Orientation Leaders

To prepare orientation leaders for the variety of tasks they are expected to perform during orientation, institutions have created rigorous training programs reflective of their orientation program goals and institutional priorities. Training programs focus on time with campus partners, group facilitation, public speaking skills, and role clarification (Payne & Sedotti, 2014). Team building and facilitating social connections are also critical components of the orientation leader role and commonly emphasized during training.

Training programs can be tied to a student leadership course or conducted as standalone training workshops ranging from a half-day to up to three weeks in duration. Among ISPL-US respondents who had served in orientation roles, 19.5% indicated their training consisted of enrolling in a mandatory class. Formal orientation leader training courses may be designed to extend across a full semester or be condensed into a half-semester experience. While some training courses are graded, it is more common for orientation leader training courses to be administered on a pass/fail system (Payne & Sedotti, 2014). Pre-service training conducted via an academic course allows for more training time with campus partners, extended opportunities for students to practice facilitation and public speaking skills, more frequent one-on-one meetings with orientation staff for more personalized development and feedback, and time for reflection on what orientation leaders are learning and how they will apply the skills they have learned. Concurrent training courses may also be offered but are far less common.

Other training programs may be standalone programs that last anywhere from a half day up to three weeks. Table 3.2 shows the distribution of training duration as reported in the ISPL-US.

Table 3.2

Orientation Leader Training Duration (n = 236)

Length	Freq.	%
Half day or less	42	17.8
1 day	57	24.2
2 days	44	18.6
1 week	52	22.0
2 weeks	51	21.6
3 weeks	24	10.2

Note. Respondents were instructed to consider all the orientation roles they had held during college and to "select all that apply"; consequently, overall table percentages exceed 100%.

To plan and determine the best approach to training orientation leaders, professional staff should review the program type, the duration of the program or number of orientation sessions, and the needs of the orientation leader role, along with what resources are allotted, and the compensation structure of the student staff (Payne & Sedotti, 2014). For many institutions, available resources are a constraining factor when it comes to orientation leader training programs. In these cases, well-designed short programs can be effective. While shorter training programs do not allow as much time for reflection, when well-designed, they can still develop orientation leaders' skills and knowledge to a level sufficient to perform essential tasks.

The Outcomes and Impact of Serving as an Orientation Leader

While orientation leaders add value to the experience of new students, serving as an orientation leader yields tremendous benefits for the orientation leaders themselves. In the discussion that follows, we will use selected results from the ISPL-US to explore how orientation leaders who responded to the survey were impacted by their experiences. We will begin by discussing demographic trends among those who serve as orientation leaders. This is a critical consideration as institutions have an obligation to make meaningful experiential learning opportunities available to all students on their campuses.

Orientation Leader Demographics

Of the students who completed the ISPL-US, 265 students identified as having served as an orientation leader or outdoor orientation leader. Table 3.3 summarizes key demographic information for those who identified as orientation leaders.

Overall, orientation leader respondents to the ISPL-US tended to be highly involved, high academic achievers, and often maintain several roles on campus. For example, respondents who had or were currently serving as orientation leaders also reported involvement in other PL roles, including student clubs or organizations (34.7%), academic roles (e.g., supplemental instruction leaders, tutors, teaching assistants; 68.6%). Additionally, 30.1% of orientation leaders who completed the survey reported that they had been involved in three or more peer leadership roles during their time in college. Finally, orientation leaders in the survey were typically working toward degrees focused in the social sciences and reported that getting to work with people was a primary driver in why they wanted to serve as an orientation leader.

Table 3.3

Demographic Profile of Orientation Leaders

Description	Freq.	%
Class Standing (n=248)		
First-Year Student	6	2.4
Second-Year Student	73	29.4
Third-Year Student	71	28.6
Fourth-Year Student	73	29.4
GPA (n=244)		
< 2.00	0	0.0
2.00 - 3.49	67	27.5
> 3.50	177	72.5
Social Class (n=248)		
Pell-eligible	71	28.6
First-generation	44	17.7
Gender (n=248)		
Agender	1	0.4
Man	59	23.8
Woman	181	73.0
Nonbinary/Genderqueer/Genderfluid	6	2.4
Prefer not to say	1	0.4
Race or Ethnicity (n_240)		
American Indian or Alaska Native	1	0.4
Asian or Asian American	16	6.5
Black or African American	20	8.1
Hispanic, Chicano/a, or Latino/a	39	15.7
Native Hawaiian or other Pacific Islander	1	0.4
White	184	74.2

Benefits of Serving as an Orientation Leader: The Orientation Leader Role as a High-Impact Practice

Rooted in the eight key characteristics of HIPs (Kuh & O'Donnell, 2013) as referenced in Chapter 1, the ISPL-US prompted orientation leaders to gauge their growth within these key elements of experience. Results of the ISPL-US provided evidence that the orientation leader experience aligns with many of the characteristics of HIPs (see Chapter 1) and provides a multitude of benefits to those students serving in the orientation leader role.

Overarchingly, orientation programs typically have goals and outcomes related to both academic and social integration (Mann et al., 2010), thus, it was no surprise that orientation leaders responding to the ISPL-US indicated growth in these areas. For instance, 42.6% of orientation leader respondents indicated an increase in their academic skills, and 82.1% reported that being an orientation leader had increased their interpersonal communication skills.

Orientation leader programs are deeply rooted in reflection and provide frequent opportunities for orientation leaders to integrate and apply their learning. For example, 81.9% of respondents reported regular reflective conversations with a supervisor, 57.2% of respondents reported regular reflective conversations with a senior PL, and 84.9% of orientation leaders who participated in the survey reported reflective opportunities as part of group discussions. Finally, orientation leaders have frequent opportunities to publicly share their learning and demonstrate competence as they participate in panels, talk in front of groups of students and their families, and make various other orientation presentations. Accordingly, 64% of respondents indicated their presentation skills improved by serving as an orientation leader.

While orientation leaders have responsibilities related to supporting both new students' academic and social integration, results of the ISPL-US showed orientation leaders themselves tend to experience more benefits related to social integration. For example, 56.8% of orientation leaders indicated increased meaningful interactions with faculty, 62.4% with staff, 79.9% with peers, and 91.5% gained increased knowledge of the institution. In contrast, only 42.6% of orientation leaders reported that their academic skills had increased because of serving as an orientation leader. Similarly, 16.1% of respondents in orientation leader roles indicated an increase in their academic performance in association with their role.

Another important characteristic of a HIP is exposure to and experiences with people and circumstances that differ from those with which students are familiar (Kuh & O'Donnell, 2013). The results of the ISPL-US also provided evidence that being an orientation leader enhanced respondents exposure to, interaction with, and learning from, others with a rich range of backgrounds. Approximately 75% of orientation leaders reported improved knowledge of, understanding of, and interactions with, people with backgrounds different than their own. This aligns with findings from Gruszka et al. (2019) that demonstrated that students in orientation leader roles experienced growth in the appreciation of differences.

Orientation Leaders' Sense of Belonging

Students' belonging and mattering has become widely studied with its connection to retention and graduation rates of undergraduate students. Strayhorn (2019) defines sense of belonging as,

> Refers to students' perceived social support on campus, a feeling or sensation of connectedness, and the experience of mattering or feeling cared about, accepted, respected, valued by, and important to the campus community or others on campus such as faculty, staff, and peers. (p. 4)

Findings from the ISPL-US also suggest that serving as an orientation leader can enhance student leaders' sense of belonging in these ways by providing valuable opportunities to interact with faculty and peers about substantive matters—an additional characteristic of HIPs (Kuh & O'Donnell, 2013). These connections that orientation leaders establish with faculty and peers are important in building a strong sense of belonging (Kirby & Thomas, 2022).

For example, 79.9% of orientation leaders reported that serving in an orientation leader role provided opportunities for meaningful interactions with peers and 62.4% reported having more meaningful interactions with staff. These findings align with the study by Camerato et al. (2019) on students participating in extra or cocurricular activities where the authors found that students who participated in leadership roles in university-wide programs like orientation experiences, described "positive feelings and meaning attached to belonging to groups or staff" (p. 65).

Orientation leaders in the ISPL-US not only reported increases in their meaningful interpersonal interactions, but they also reported gains related to their more general sense of belonging and connection to the broader campus. Indeed, 72% of orientation leader respondents reported an increased feeling of belonging to campus, while 65.6% reported an increased desire to stay at the institution and graduate. Finally, connection to the institution can also be related to awareness of resources available and 91.5% reported improved knowledge of campus resources. In summary, both findings from the ISPL-US as well as previous research on the orientation leader experience offer evidence that serving as an orientation leader is associated with an improved sense of belonging.

CAS Standards and Orientation Leader Programs

CAS maintains recommendations for intentionally designed orientation leader training and new student orientation programs (NSOPs). Many of these recommendations align with the characteristics of HIPs. In what follows we analyze the findings of the ISPL-US related to orientation leader experiences through the framework of the CAS standards.

The first standard from CAS (2023) that aligns with the ISPL-US states, "NSOPs must design and facilitate intentional opportunities for new students to interact with other new students as well as continuing students, faculty, and staff members" (p. 7). Results of the ISPL-US provide evidence that this standard is largely being met for the orientation leaders who participated in the study, with 79.9% reporting that being an orientation leader increased their meaningful interactions with peers, 56.8% reporting that their meaningful interactions with faculty increased, and 62.4% reporting that being an orientation leader increased their meaningful interactions with staff. As described previously in this chapter, serving as an orientation leader seems to offer powerful opportunities for meaningful interactions with others in the campus community.

An additional CAS standard (2023) that can be analyzed using ISPL-US data states that "undergraduate and graduate student employees working in NSOP must be carefully selected, trained, supervised, and evaluated by supervisors with applicable educational credentials, work experience, and supervisory experience" (p. 16). Additionally, "NSOP must train orientation student staff and other paraprofessionals on ways to support the mission and goals of NSOP and the institution" (CAS, 2023, p. 16). Of the orientation leader respondents to the ISPL-US, 52.9% indicated they "applied for, and [were] interviewed for the position/[were] subsequently appointed." Additionally, as outlined in Table 3.2, respondents in orientation roles reported at least one of their orientation roles required a high degree of training and preparation. Indeed, 24.2% of orientation leader respondents indicated that they had completed one day of training, 22.0% reporting one week of training, 21.6% reporting two weeks of training, and 19.5% reporting that at least one of their orientation roles required enrollment in a mandatory class. We note that CAS standards for orientation programs do not recommend any length of training but only that the training provided be adequate for the particular orientation leader role.

An additional aspect of training and preparation involves the feedback that orientation leaders receive. Results of the ISPL-US suggest that this was a regular part of the experience for most of the orientation leaders who participated in the study. Indeed, 66.8% of respondents indicated they received feedback on their performance as an orientation leader. This evaluation process is both part of the NSOP standards (CAS, 2023) and a critical component of HIPs (Kuh & O'Donnell, 2013).

One area in which orientation programs might improve relates to the CAS standard (2023) that outlines, "NSOP undergraduate and graduate student employees must be representative of the institution's student body, reflecting the diversity of the institutional community" (p. 17). As discussed earlier in the chapter, orientation leaders who participated in the 2023 ISPL-US study were predominantly White, continuing generation women. While we do not have data on the demographic makeup of the institutions who participated in the study, orientation leader respondents did not appear to be overly diverse. Practitioners should take care to ensure their orientation leaders reflect their institutional demographics and work to provide access to the orientation leader experience for a wide range of students.

The *NODA: Association for Orientation, Transition, and Retention Orientation Planning Manual* (2014) provides guidance for orientation staff selection processes and for training. Payne and Sedotti (2014) encouraged practitioners to consider the "purpose of the student staff; timing of the orientation program; length of the orientation period; influence and authority of student staff; compensation; and time and resources you have for training" (pp. 80-81). These parameters will help determine both the design of the selection process, as well as the type of training that is best suited for the institution's orientation program.

Finally, based on responses to the ISPL-US, orientation leader programs are proving successful in helping students develop several different leadership and soft skills, with 96.0% of orientation leader respondents indicating that serving as an orientation leader improved their general leadership skills. Table 3.4 shows students' perceptions of the orientation leader role's impact on specific aspects of their leadership skill development.

Table 3.4

Impact of Orientation Leader Experience on Skill Development

Skill	Freq.	%
Teamwork and collaboration (*n*=235)	218	92.8
Interpersonal communication (*n*=235)	222	94.4
Written communication (*n*=234)	172	73.5
Presentation (*n*=233)	192	82.4
Problem solving (*n*=234)	199	85.0
Decision making (*n*=234)	199	89.3
Adaptability (*n*=234)	209	89.3
Creativity (*n*=235)	190	80.9

Recommendations for Practitioners

Based on the data gathered from students who had served in an orientation leader role, we identified several gaps in the orientation leader experience. Following, we discuss practical recommendations related to issues of diversity, equity, inclusion in the orientation leader role; access to orientation leader experiences; as well as how the orientation leader experience could be redesigned to better contribute to academic and social integration. Ultimately, these recommendations are meant to help the orientation leader experience better align with CAS standards (2023) and the characteristics of HIPs (Kuh & O'Donnell, 2013).

Despite providing strong evidence related to the benefits that come to students serving in the orientation leader role, the results of the ISPL-US also pointed to several opportunities to refine or change program frameworks to focus on holistic student success, beyond only social integration. Indeed, only 16.1% of orientation leader respondents indicated improvement in their academic performance based on their experiences within the orientation leader role. Additionally, only 13.5% indicated that being an orientation leader increased their GPA, and just 13.9% responded that the orientation leader experience increased the number of credit hours they earned each semester. As reported previously, 73% of respondents reported a GPA between 3.5 and 4.0. Consequently, these percentages may be lower simply because these leaders were high academic achievers prior to being selected for an orientation leader role, resulting in a ceiling effect relative to being an orientation leader and increasing one's GPA.

Similarly, while a large percentage of orientation leader respondents reported that being an orientation leader improved their interactions with peers and staff, a far lower percentage (56.8%) reported improved interactions with faculty because of their orientation leader experiences. This may be because some orientation programs do not offer substantive opportunities for faculty to be involved. However, given the importance of students' connection to faculty during times of transition, this leaves significant room for improvement relative to the ways in which faculty are invited to participate in orientation events and programming. We recommend practitioners consider how increased faculty involvement in orientation or orientation leader training could both enhance orientation programming and provide added benefit to the leaders in these roles. A study conducted by Kirby and Thomas (2022) demonstrated the impact faculty and instructors who are perceived as "caring, supportive, competent, and good communicators" (p. 375) have in creating an environment where students feel more connected to instructors. Faculty participating in orientation through presentations, lectures, activities, or less formal meet and greets, can help nurture these relationships before classes start and provide both new students and orientation leaders with increased comfort in interacting with faculty members as students move forward.

Barriers to Access to the Orientation Leader Role

As mentioned earlier in the chapter, a key consideration for practitioners is the diversity of the orientation leader team and ensuring that equal access to these roles is provided for all students. The team should be reflective of the overall student population. This gives incoming students an opportunity to see themselves in the role and see themselves in the student body of the campus. One purpose of the orientation leader position is to serve as a role model, so essentially recruitment for the next team of orientation leaders begins during the orientation program.

The demographics of students serving as orientation leaders highlighted earlier showed potential inequities and barriers to access to the position. For example, the percentage of first-generation students participating in orientation leader roles seems to be relatively low, based on the results of the ISPL-US. Practitioners should consider the makeup of their team and potential barriers especially when recruiting marginalized and minoritized applicants and developing the overall job experience, including minimum requirements, length or duration of employment, and compensation. An additional way to address issues of access is to ensure that orientation leaders are adequately compensated for their work. We were somewhat discouraged that nearly half (48.8%) of the ISPL-US respondents who had served in orientation roles indicated that at least one of these roles was completely voluntary. When orientation leader roles are purely voluntary, students with financial need are highly likely to choose not to apply or accept positions given the large amount of time required to satisfy job requirements.

All students should have access to the benefits of serving in a peer leadership role. Practitioners who employ orientation leaders should review the demographics of students filling those positions and consider recruitment strategies that can diversify the hiring pool. For example, orientation directors could collaborate with academic or student service departments that serve marginalized populations to review the position to identify potential barriers to access, as well as recruit PLs representing a range of identities.

An additional recommendation for practitioners includes reconsideration of minimum requirements for the position. Given the purpose of orientation programs to assist students with their academic and social integration to campus, practitioners often formulate the orientation leader program to recruit students who have had ongoing success both socially and academically and are able to role model and assist new students in achieving that success. However, practitioners could reconceptualize their approach to recruitment by targeting students who may have initially struggled to transition to their campus, but who have overcome challenges and are working toward thriving. By designing high-quality training and providing necessary support, campuses can have confidence that a combination of thoughtful selection and training can yield a pool of orientation leaders who are both qualified and resilient. Indeed, students who have overcome challenges academically or socially can share what they have learned with future students, connect them with key resources, and take an empathic approach in supporting students in transition.

Compensation and housing availability are additional considerations for orientation directors and staff. If the position is a volunteer role, clearly setting that expectation at the outset of recruitment and hiring is important. Even in a volunteer position, meals, uniforms, and other resources or swag can open access for a wider segment of students. Practitioners should consider the type of orientation program they run and consider the ethicality and risks of orientation models that do not provide compensation for orientation leaders.

A clear, consistent schedule for training and for orientation events also helps students who may also need to be concurrently enrolled in classes during orientation season, or students who will be working in additional jobs to meet financial need. Since these positions frequently involve summertime work (when many students may need to be earning income for the following academic year), professional staff must consider the structure of their orientation leader roles, including wages, housing accommodations, the number of hours offered to orientation leaders, etc. Similarly, in a paid position, professional staff need to use the recruitment and hiring process to ensure that applicants clearly understand how many hours they are expected to work each week. For students with high financial need and who need to work full-time during the summer, this is vital as they make plans and decisions.

Housing is another consideration for the position. If institutions can provide housing, including gap housing after the spring semester and after orientation programs have concluded, this provides the most equal access for all orientation leaders. Institutions that do not have overnight orientation, that can permit students to opt in to housing, also cast a wide net in attracting a variety of students for the position. Many prospective orientation leaders may already have signed leases for off-campus housing, or are adult learners with young children, so having non-overnight options opens access to the orientation leader role to a wider range of students at the institution.

Implications for Future Research

There is need for additional research that explores the unique experiences of orientation leaders with various identities. Additionally, there is limited research on the recruitment, hiring, and training of orientation leaders, along with their experience overall and its direct impact on sense of belonging, retention, GPA, or even graduation of these students, in comparison to their non-orientation leader peers.

Although the data from the ISPL-US provide understanding of the experiences of those students who serve in orientation leader roles, there are obvious limitations to self-reported data. Future research should focus on collecting direct measures of academic performance among orientation leaders to provide understanding of how academic performance is impacted over time, as well as how serving as an orientation leader impacts a student's likelihood to persist to graduation. Similarly, it would be helpful to compare the self-reported data from the ISPL-US to direct measures of academic skill development to provide stronger evidence of whether specific skills truly improved. Finally, future studies could research the direct impacts of serving as an orientation leader on sense of belonging and social integration. In sum, the ISPL-US data provides an important starting point for understanding the experiences of students who serve in orientation roles and helpful guidance for orientation practitioners to use for both program improvement and future publishable research.

Case Study: Application of Data

The case study described below provides an opportunity to process the data reported on and analyzed in this chapter. The study is followed by recommendations for practitioners.

Case Study

Southeast University is a predominantly White institution in the suburbs outside of a major city. The university enrolls over 25,000 students. The incoming class each year typically consists of approximately 4,000 new first-year students and 1,000 transfer students and is trending toward a majority-minority population. The percentages of first-generation and Pell-eligible students who make up the first-year class are also increasing. The new student orientation program is a one-day model, held four times per week, across June and July. Additionally, Southeast University also offers a Welcome Week program with required sessions immediately before classes start in August.

The orientation leader position is a paid, stipend position for the summer. Orientation leaders are hired in the previous fall semester and participate in a full semester training course during the spring semester. Orientation leaders often need to pay for the one-credit course as it brings them above the allotted course load. Orientation leaders are not paid for the semester course as it is credit bearing. Orientation leaders also complete an additional two weeks of required summer training that includes a financial stipend. Housing is not included for the orientation leaders but is available at a nightly rate.

The orientation leader position requires that students work all orientation sessions. They cannot take any summer classes because of the duration and intensity of training and the high number of orientation sessions held during June and July. Their contract is for up to 40 hours per week and offers a monetary stipend. You have been told that the orientation leaders often use the amount of their stipend and the number of hours they work to determine that their compensation falls below minimum wage.

Orientation leaders are responsible for a small group of 15 students during each orientation session. They also serve on panels during the program and participate in the orientation welcome. Once the summer programs are complete, their job is complete, and they have no role during the Welcome Week or throughout the fall semester.

Consider and address the following questions:

- In what ways does the orientation leader position align with the type of orientation offered and the characteristics of Southeast University?

- What changes would you make to the position to make it more accessible to all students? What considerations might you need to make for first-generation college students? What about students who identify as members of any other minoritized or marginalized communities? What are the implications of this model of orientation for low-income students?

- What changes would you make to the orientation leader position to better align it with the institutional culture and characteristics of its students?

- How could this position be reworked to optimize student learning and skill development?

Considerations for Practitioners

There are several ways in which Southeast University could adjust their orientation leader practices to make the position more accessible to students. Some initial adjustments to the position could include an evaluation of the amount of the stipend, in comparison to the average number of hours worked by orientation leaders. Orientation leaders should receive a fair wage that acknowledges the total amount of time they devote to their role from their hiring until the summer's end. Additionally, the university could more clearly describe the additional benefits the orientation leader can expect to receive. One of those benefits could be providing their housing and some or all meals through the duration of the orientation programs. Southeast should work to partner with their colleagues in Housing to determine if providing free, or even reduced, housing costs could be possible. Orientation leaders could then be given the option of determining whether they want to live on campus or make alternative off-campus arrangements.

Another barrier to access is the academic cost. The staff at Southeast University should review their training course to determine its effectiveness and how many of their orientation leaders must pay for the credit. They should work to have the cost of the course covered for students. An additional academic barrier is the inability to take courses over the orientation period. Southeast University staff should review this policy to determine ways that students could take an online class, an evening class, or a class that does not overlap with the orientation schedule. The staff should be informed by the orientation leaders what class(es) they are taking to help avoid any conflicts and to better position staff to support orientation leaders in their academic experience.

To help orientation leaders experience deeper learning from their experiences, Southeast University should examine the conclusion of the orientation leader role. They can help the orientation leaders synthesize what they learned from participating in this PL position and identify how what they have learned could position them for future leadership roles, employment opportunities, etc.

Also, program leaders could examine how orientation leaders might be integrated into welcome week programming or existing structures for providing support to new students through the first few weeks of the semester. After all, orientation leaders tend to develop strong relationships with their students during orientation and these relationships could be leveraged to provide additional opportunities for orientation leaders serve as role models and facilitate belonging for new students across their transition experiences and beyond formal orientation events.

The nature of the orientation position, no matter the orientation model, has some inherent barriers. The position is often a short duration, highly intense position. The recruiting materials should reflect the nature of the job, the benefits students can expect, and what the student will get out of participating in a peer leadership role. This will help recruit students who sincerely want to help incoming students and who would also benefit from serving in the orientation leader role.

Conclusion

The 2023 ISPL-US provided the opportunity for students serving in the capacity of an orientation leader to reflect on their role and provide critical data for practitioners and researchers. Based on their responses, the orientation leader experience does seem to align with many of the characteristics of HIPs, such as opportunities for real-world application, exposure to and experience with people of differing backgrounds, quality interactions with faculty and staff, critical feedback and reflection, and public demonstration of learning. Given the broad variation in orientation leader roles, additional studies could help explore how various elements of the experience—training, feedback, and reflection—are integrated into the program and impact orientation leaders' learning and growth. Also, future research could help develop frameworks that provide guidance for how orientation professionals can align training, feedback, and reflection with learning outcomes geared toward student skill and leadership development. Practitioners in the field of orientation, transition, and retention could then use this framework to help intentionally develop their orientation leader program to set these expectations and further grow and measure the skill development that occurs based on students' participation in the role. The results of the ISPL-US were strong indicators that significant growth is occurring across several social, academic, and leadership skills and that students benefit in several dimensions by having served as an orientation leader.

References

Bristow, D. (2014). Orientation staff selection. In *NODA Orientation Planning Manual.* https://nodaconnect.nodaweb.org/viewdocument/orientation-planning-manual-2014

Camerato, K., Clift, A., Golden, M. N., Vivas, J. G., Rogers, P., & Strelecki, A. (2019). What does "high-impact" mean in extracurricular experiences? *Journal of Campus Activities Practice and Scholarship, 1*(1), 60-67. https://eric.ed.gov/?id=EJ1359545

Council for the Advancement of Standards in Higher Education (2023). *CAS professional standards for higher education.* https://www.cas.edu/standards.html

Greenfield, G. M., Keup, J. R., & Gardner, J. N. (2013). *Developing and sustaining successful first-year programs: A guide for practitioners* (1st ed.). Jossey-Bass.

Gruszka, L., Witt, E., & Tower, E. (2019). Longitudinal comparison of orientation leader learning outcomes. *Journal of College Orientation, Transition, and Retention, 26*(2). https://doi.org/10.24926/jcotr.v26i2.2398

Kirby, L. A. J., & Thomas, C. L. (2022). High-impact teaching practices foster a greater sense of belonging in the college classroom, *Journal of Further and Higher Education, 46*(3), 368-381. https://doi.org/10.1080/0309877X.2021.1950659

Kuh, G. D., & O'Donnell, K. (2013). Ensuring quality and taking high-impact practices to scale. *Peer Review, 15*(2), 32-33.

Mack, C. E. (2010). A brief overview of the orientation, transition, and retention field. In J. A. Ward-Roof (Ed.), *Designing successful transitions: A guide for orienting students to college* (Monograph No. 13, 3rd ed., pp. 3-10). University of South Carolina, National Resource Center for The First-Year Experience and Students in Transition.

Mann, A., Andrews, C., & Rodenburg, N. (2010). Administration of a comprehensive orientation program. In J. A. Ward-Roof (Ed.), *Designing successful transitions: A guide for orienting student to college* (3rd ed., pp. 43-60). University of South Carolina, National Resource Center for The First-Year Experience and Students in Transition.

NODA. (2017). *NODA Databank Survey 2017.* https://nodaconnect.nodaweb.org/communities/community-home/librarydocuments?LibraryKey=7c6cd4bb-ddf2-4d55-9d16-018d439ea83f&LibraryFolderKey=8fdf07a2-95c0-4905-98b8-018d43dfe041

Payne, M. & Sedotti, M. (2014). Orientation staff training. In *NODA orientation planning manual.* https://nodaconnect.nodaweb.org/viewdocument/orientation-planning-manual-2014

Rode, D. L., & Wolfman, A. (2014). New student orientation. In *NODA orientation planning Manual.* https://nodaconnect.nodaweb.org/viewdocument/orientation-planning-manual-2014

Strayhorn, T. L. (2019). *College students' sense of belonging: A key to educational success for all students* (2nd ed.). Routledge.

Upcraft, M. L., Gardner, J. N., Barefoot, B. O., & Associates. (2005). *Challenging and supporting the first-year student: A handbook for improving the first year of college.* Jossey-Bass.

Young, D. G. (Ed.). (2019). *2017 National survey on the first-year experience: Creating and coordinating structures to support student success.* University of South Carolina.

Chapter 4

Are Times A-Changing? The Complicated Role of the Resident Assistant as Peer Leader

Tori Negash
Association of College & University Housing Officers-International (ACUHO-I)

Resident Assistants (RAs) are integral members of residence life departments at higher education institutions across the United States. As peer leaders (PLs) within this area of college life, they live alongside the students they serve in campus housing. The responsibilities of the RA role have expanded and become more complex over time, with expectations of meeting the needs of their peers 24 hours a day, 365 days a year. While there are rich benefits both to living on campus and serving as an RA, including exposure to high-impact practices (HIPs) and growth in skills and employability outcomes, the complicated nature of the role can lead to increased feelings of stress and burnout that negatively affect well-being. Discussions around whether the RA position should be re-envisioned have emerged in the last decade and gained momentum in recent years. In fact, in 2021 (GW Today, 2021), George Washington University (GWU) decided to take this from theoretical to tangible and deployed re-envisioned student positions on campus, aiming to continue providing the defining experiences associated with serving as an RA, while mitigating the potential causes of stress, burnout, and negative outcomes among this unique PL group.

This chapter provides a brief overview of residence life and the RA role. I have also offered research regarding the experiences of RAs from minoritized identities as context for understanding how students experience the peer leadership role differently based on identity. I will discuss the idea of re-envisioning the RA role, including how this could impact students, and what this might look like in action. Readers will also find a case study highlighting changes to the RA role at GWU at the end of this chapter. Key findings from the 2023 ISPL-US regarding RAs and residence life are discussed; throughout the results sections, links to HIPs and additional data from the Campus Housing Index (CHI; 2023b), a data benchmarking tool from the Association of College and University Housing Officers – International (ACUHO-I), are incorporated where appropriate. The chapter concludes with recommendations for next steps and avenues for future research.

Residence Life and Resident Assistants: The Who, What, When, Where, and Why

Residence life is a holistic term encompassing the overall experience of living in college or university housing such as dormitories, apartments, fraternity and sorority houses, or other university-owned or sponsored housing. Residence life is also a department, or a function of a department, within a college or university (McClure, et al., 2022). Residence life stands apart on campuses, as its purpose is to address "all of a student's life experiences" (McClure, et al., 2022, p. 73). University housing has evolved into communities that support students' learning, development, and well-being (Manata et al., 2017). Housing and residence life professionals, including both full- and part-time professional staff and student employees, are on the front line of ensuring students have meaningful experiences and successfully navigate living away from home (Fassett et al., 2021).

RAs are integral student leaders on college and university campuses (Martin & Blechschmidt, 2014). They are also in the unique position to occupy a role that is designed to benefit both the residential community and them (McClure et al., 2022), as living on campus is frequently cited as having a positive impact on student academic outcomes (Fassett et al., 2021; Graham et al., 2018), and the development of a student's sense of belonging, identity formation, and engagement with their community (Strange & Banning, 2015). The duties RAs fulfill through this position are critical to the functioning of housing and residence life units (Hernandez & Smith, 2019); however, the role and its responsibilities are also ever evolving and increasingly complex (Boone et al., 2016; McClure et al., 2022; Soria & Roberts, 2023). As of the 2021-2022 academic year, 10 areas of primary responsibility for the RA position had been identified through the CHI; these include interactions with residents, duty, community development, policy enforcement/safety, programming, crisis response, wellness checks, peer mentoring, facility management, and front desk duty (ACUHO-I, 2023b). Given the growing list of responsibilities, and in an attempt to lessen feelings of stress and burnout amongst RAs, some institutions have started making changes to the position and its function within residence life. Examples include removing the requirement to work the residence hall front desk, using predesigned bulletin boards rather than creating from scratch, and segmenting RA responsibilities so students serve one distinct role rather than many (Walker, 2022). Further discussion of these changes, and their implementation at one university, are discussed at the end of this chapter.

Experience of Resident Assistants from Minoritized Identity Groups

Campus housing is often a primary setting for students to interact with people and circumstances that differ from those with which they are familiar, perhaps for the first time (Fosnacht et al., 2020). Research has shown that among college students, these experiences lead to growth in learning outcomes and critical thinking skills (Nelson Laird et al., 2005). RAs live among those they are asked to supervise and lead (Foste & Johnson, 2021), an aspect of the role that sets it apart from other peer leadership positions in higher education. Living where you work is a highly immersive and demanding experience, and one that can lead to a blurring of the line between personal and professional. For RAs from minoritized identity groups, we must consider how their identities affect their experience as both resident and leader (Foste & Johnson, 2021).

RAs with minoritized identities report facing heightened scrutiny of their job performance from residents, supervisors, and peer RAs from dominant identity groups (Schuster & Stalker, 2022). This aspect of their experience may lead to a desire to combat stereotypes and unfair expectations, often through outperforming aspects of the position (Schuster & Stalker, 2022). As leaders on campus who also represent minoritized groups, they may be identified by their peers, other RAs, or staff and administrators as token members of the group(s) they identify with (Schuster & Stalker, 2022), or asked to promote institutional messaging contrary to their lived experiences (Linley, 2018). While all RAs experience stress, burnout, and secondary trauma to some degree (Correa et al., 2023), these may be intensified for RAs with minoritized identities (Foste & Johnson, 2021; Schuster & Stalker, 2022). The research highlighted here does not negate the potential for positive outcomes among RAs, but, rather, suggests that barriers to accessing these outcomes within housing and residence life exist. Identity-affirming environments have the potential to support growth and development among all students (Schuster, 2023); intentionally creating environments that foster positive outcomes must be a continual effort by all campus stakeholders (Mollett et al., 2021).

Key Findings Related to the RA Peer Leadership Experience

Results of the 2023 ISPL-US provide insight into key aspects of who RAs are, their motivations for seeking the role, the support they receive through training and for mental health and well-being, details of the position, and the impact serving in this role has on the student.

Resident Assistant Demographics

Most RAs (33.6%) were second-year students, followed by third year (28.1%) and fourth year (24.7%). While subject areas varied, the top three majors reported were social sciences (18.7%), health professions and related programs (16.6%), and business, management, marketing, and related support services (15.3%). Overall, 95.3% of RAs reported a GPA of 3.00 or higher. Virtually all RAs fell within the 18-25 age range (99%), with near equal representation between the 18-20 (49.8%) and 21-25 (49.4%) groups. One in five RAs (20.9%) was a first-generation college student and nearly 30% were Pell Grant eligible (29.4%). Most identified as a woman (68.1%; see Table 4.1), and as White (77%; see Table 4.2), both of which are consistent with overall ISPL-US data. About six in 10 (63.4%) were in-state students, while less than 2% were international students.

Table 4.1

Gender Identity of Students in an RA Peer Leadership Role (n = 235)

	RAs	
Gender	**Freq.**	**%**
Agender	1	0.4
Man	55	23.4
Woman	160	68.1
Nonbinary/Genderqueer/Genderfluid	15	6.4
Two Spirit	0	0.0
Another identity	2	0.9
Prefer not to say	2	0.9

Table 4.2

Race or Ethnicity of Students in an RA Peer Leadership Role (n = 235)

	RAs	
Race of Ethnicity	**Freq.**	**%**
American Indian or Alaska Native	4	1.7
Asian or Asian American	18	7.7
Black or African American	21	8.9
Hispanic, Chicano/a, or Latino/a	30	12.8
Native Hawaiian or other Pacific Islander	5	2.1
White	181	77.0
Other	5	2.1
Prefer not to say	2	0.9

RA Position Details

Most RAs (52.7%) reported serving in only that role, but about one in four (25.7%) served in two PL roles, and 14.9% served in three. About one in three students (32.3%) served as an academic peer mentor (e.g., peer advisor, tutor, supplemental instruction leader, etc.) in addition to their RA position; other roles included clubs or organizations (23%), first-year experience (19.6%), and campus activities (17.4%). Students most often served as an RA for one (28.6%) or two (25.2%) semesters. Data from the CHI are similar, with an average of two semesters during the 2021-2022 academic year (ACUHO-I, 2023b). In terms of hours worked per week, 32.8% of RAs reported working 16-20 hours per week, on average, in that role; again, CHI data are similar, with an average of 17 hours per week (ACUHO-I, 2023b).

There was variation in compensation received among RAs; as a "select all that apply" question, percentages will not equal 100. Financial compensation included:

- An hourly wage or stipend: 82.7%,
- Residential room and board reduction: 87.3%,
- Financial aid such as a scholarship: 7.3%,
- Fees reduction: 4.1%, and
- Gift cards, vouchers, other gifts: 6.4%

Other compensation was course credit (30%) and acknowledgement on their academic transcript (6.4%). More than one in four RAs (27.3%) reported their position as volunteer, therefore not receiving any form of compensation.

Motivations to Serve as an RA

As seen in Table 4.3, students identified the factors that motivated them to take on their peer leadership role(s). For students serving as RAs, the factors varied, with eight of the 12 selected by over half of the students. The top motivator was helping or benefiting other students (84%), followed by personal/professional challenges, and skill development (76%).

Table 4.3

Factors that Motivated Students to Take on the RA Peer Leadership Role (n = 225)

	RAs	
Motivation	**Freq.**	**%**
To help or benefit others	189	84.0
For personal/professional challenges and skill development	171	76.0
To earn an income while studying	158	70.2
To share my knowledge/expertise with others	149	66.2
To receive reduced study/accommodation fees	133	59.1
To be more involved in the University community and meet new people	131	58.2
For the enjoyment/experience	128	56.9
For current or future job prospects	121	53.8
To give back to or serve the University	67	29.8
For academic development – improve my subject knowledge	49	21.8
To be more involved in academic/governance aspects of the University	23	10.2
Other	6	2.7

Note. Students could select all answers that applied to them for this question. As a result, the frequencies will not total the sample size and percentages will not total 100.

The Resident Assistant Experience: Workforce Development, Training, and Skills Development

Students highly rated the RA experience, with 87.5% slightly to very satisfied. More than nine in 10 (93.3%) reported they would recommend being a PL to other students; 60.6% responded they would absolutely recommend it.

Training

RAs reported varied types of training for their position. Nearly six in 10 (59.6%) received initial training for all their peer leadership positions, while 30.2% received this initial training for only most of their positions. This initial training most often lasted two weeks (45%), but students also reported one-week training (30.5%) or enrollment in a mandatory class (32.7%). A high percentage of RAs (87.7%) reported ongoing training through staff meetings (77.1%), workshops (75.5%), meetings with a supervisor (49.5%), or periodic refresher sessions prior to or during the semester (42.2%). The receipt of ongoing, formal training is related to the HIPs of structured opportunities to reflect and integrate learning, interactions with faculty and peers about substantive matters, and interactions with people and circumstances that differ from those with which students are familiar.

Supervision and Performance Feedback

Students reported receiving supervision, performance feedback, and opportunities for reflection throughout their time as an RA; these align with the HIPs of performance expectations set at appropriately high levels; frequent, timely, and constructive feedback; and periodic, and structured opportunities to reflect and integrate learning. Nearly nine in 10 students (87.8%) reported receiving feedback at regular intervals; most often through meetings with a supervising staff or faculty member (91.2%), or surveys, questionnaires, or evaluations completed by students from their floor or building (56.2%). Most RAs (79.6%) reported regular opportunities to reflect on, articulate, and integrate their learning through regular conversations with a supervisor (90.9%), group discussions during training with other RAs (67.4%), and written reflections, such as journals, or weekly or end of semester reports (52%).

Skill Development

Students identified skills further developed due to their experiences as an RA. Results (see Table 4.4) highlight several HIPs, including opportunities to discover relevance of learning through real-world applications and public demonstration of competence. The greatest skill development reported was in leadership, and teamwork and collaboration, with 93% of students reporting a slight to great increase in both, respectively. Adaptability had the second highest rating, with 91.7% reporting a slight to great increase, and interpersonal communication (91.2%) a close third.

For overall academic skills, 50.7% of RAs felt these increased in some capacity but 33.2% reported no change. More than six in 10 students (62.5%) felt their ability to succeed in a full-time job after graduation had increased. When asked about specific skills typically associated with academic success, nearly nine in 10 students felt creativity (88%), problem solving (87.9%), and decision making (87.1%) increased. More than nine in 10 students (91.4%) felt that they were better able to analyze problems from a new perspective. More than eight in 10 students felt their abilities to engage in ethical decision making (84%) and apply knowledge to a real world setting through hands on experiences (89%) had increased.

Table 4.4

Skills Development Among Students Serving in an RA Peer Leadership Role

	RAs	
Skill measured	**Freq.**	**%**
Leadership Skills		
Leadership ($n = 216$)	201	93.0
Teamwork and collaboration ($n = 217$)	202	93.0
Adaptability ($n = 217$)	199	91.7
Communication Skills		
Interpersonal communication ($n = 216$)	197	91.2
Written communication (n = 216)	157	72.7
Presentation ($n = 217$)	161	74.2
Sharing ideas with others in writing ($n = 208$)	143	68.7
Provide direction through interpersonal persuasion ($n = 207$)	175	84.5
Academic Success Skills		
Overall academic skills (n = 217)	110	50.7
Creativity ($n = 217$)	191	88.0
Problem solving ($n = 215$)	189	87.9
Decision making ($n = 216$)	188	87.1
Project management ($n = 213$)	186	87.3
Critical thinking ($n = 216$)	185	85.7
Organizational skills ($n = 214$)	181	84.6
Time management skills ($n = 214$)	178	83.1
Analyze problems from new perspectives ($n = 209$)	191	91.4
Create innovative approaches to complete a task ($n = 209$)	183	87.5
Engage in ethical decision making ($n = 206$)	173	84.0
Bring together information learned in different places ($n = 208$)	181	87.0
Applying knowledge to a real-world setting through hands on experiences ($n = 209$)	186	89.0
Academics		
GPA ($n = 209$)	51	24.4
Credit hours completed each term ($n = 209$)	75	35.8
Ability to succeed in full-time job after graduation ($n = 208$)	130	62.5

Note. For each skill, percentages represent the combined total of students who responded that their ability or performance slightly increased, increased, or greatly increased.

Impact of Serving as a Resident Assistant: Diversity, Retention, and Belonging

Through the RA peer leadership experience, RAs are routinely interacting with faculty, staff, and their peers, engaging in meaningful experiences with others who are different from themselves, feeling a greater sense of belonging within their community, and feeling more connected to their institution (see Table 4.5). Growth and development in these areas align with the HIPs of interactions with faculty and peers about substantive matters, experiences with individuals of differing backgrounds, and opportunities to discover the relevance of learning through real-world applications. Through their experiences as an RA, most students felt there was a slight to great increase in meaningful interactions with faculty (65.1%), staff (86.4%), and their peers (91.9%).

Virtually every student (96.3%) reported an increase in their knowledge of campus resources. Nearly nine in 10 students (89.0%) reported feeling that their experience as an RA slightly to greatly increased their knowledge about people with backgrounds different from their own, 92.5% felt that their interactions with people with different backgrounds from their own increased slightly to greatly, and 90.5% felt that their understanding of people with backgrounds different from their own increased slightly to greatly. More than nine in 10 (91%) noted an increase in their feelings of contributing to their campus community and in their ability to build relationships with the people with whom they work (91.8%).

Table 4.5

Impact of Serving as an RA on Diversity, Retention, and Belonging Experiences

	RAs	
Type of Impact	**Freq.**	**%**
Belonging		
Meaningful interactions with faculty (*n* = 212)	138	65.1
Meaningful interactions with staff members (*n* = 212)	183	86.4
Meaningful interactions with peers (*n* = 210)	193	91.9
Knowledge of campus resources (*n* = 209)	201	96.3
Feeling that you belong and are welcome at your institution (*n* = 210)	171	81.4
Contributing to your campus community (*n* = 212)	193	91.0
Building relationships with people with whom you work (*n* = 207)	190	91.8
Retention		
Desire to stay at your institution and graduate (*n* = 211)	138	65.4
Desire to engage in continuous learning after graduation (*n* = 211)	131	62.1
Diversity & Access		
Knowledge of people with backgrounds different than your own (*n* = 209)	186	89.0
Interaction with people with backgrounds different than your own (*n* = 211)	195	92.5
Understanding of people with backgrounds different than your own (*n* = 211)	191	90.5

Note. For each skill, percentages represent the combined total of students who responded that this skill slightly increased, increased, or greatly increased.

Practical Guidance and Recommendations

As established by prior research, results of the 2023 ISPL-US demonstrate that engaging in peer leadership as an RA has a positive impact on student skills, leads to exposure to learning across and knowledge of differences, affirms a sense of belonging and place on campus, and engages students in workforce training and development that will aid them in their future beyond higher education.

These results also highlight that the experience of being an RA aligns with the characteristic of HIPs. Through experiences with people and circumstances from backgrounds that differ from their own, receiving high-quality supervision, participating in ongoing training, and having opportunities for self-reflection, RAs are routinely engaged in experiences that feature high expectations, reflection and integrated learning, frequent feedback, real world applications, exposure to diverse perspectives, and interaction with faculty and peers about substantive matters. Looking to the findings reported here, the force of these experiences may be most evident in the growth and development of specific skills and employability outcomes. While these are not necessarily a part of the day-to-day experience of an RA, the design of this peer leadership role facilitates growth in these areas.

Engaging in PL activities as an RA has a unique and impactful effect on the lives of students who serve; however, what is extraordinary about this leadership role on campus is the far-reaching impact RAs have on their peers as well. In a time of declining funding and cuts to staffing and programs, findings such as these can serve as justification for the RA position and residence life overall—making the case for why campus housing should remain a part of the student experience in higher education (ACUHO-I, 2023a).

It is worth noting, though, that the RA experience is not without its limitations. As mentioned in prior sections, there are concerns about stress, burnout, secondary trauma, and overall well-being. RAs with minoritized identities may experience these things in an even more intense way. Combating the potential for these negative outcomes, while maintaining the beneficial, high-impact aspects of this role, is vital in moving forward. As conversations around revising the RA role continue, campus leaders should weigh the findings discussed here and seriously consider how their institutions might change the RA position to include fewer responsibilities or be more specialized, while still aligning with the characteristics of HIPs.

Motivations for Seeking a Peer Leadership Role

Student motivations for seeking a PL role as an RA fell into broad categories of helping others and their community, finances, involvement in the university and community, skill development, and workforce development/career planning. Having insight into the motivations of students seeking peer leadership roles can aid institutions with their recruitment efforts. Communicating the positive effects of serving as an RA, and how those align with the motivations highlighted here, may lead to greater numbers of students applying for the role. The data discussed here help to "make the case" for not only campus housing, but for serving in the RA role. Institutions can communicate this information on their housing and residence life website, as well as through working with their institutional communications office to publish articles, share student stories and testimonials, post on social media, and otherwise highlight the positive outcomes detailed here. When RA recruitment is happening on campus, this information should be included as part of that process; this could mean adding details to flyers and advertisements posted around campus and online, inviting students who previously served as RAs to be part of the recruitment and hiring process, or intentionally discussing this information in conversations with potential RA candidates.

Importance of Ongoing Training

Once students are serving in the role, ongoing training is critical for their development as a leader and supporting them as individuals. The type of training provided may be more important than the frequency, although the right pacing is also a factor to consider. Given the varied identities and experiences of the students serving in this role, campuses should avoid a one-size-fits-all approach. Having an infrastructure for providing ongoing training in place, with funding and staff allocated to these efforts, is key. However, institutions should tailor the specifics of the training to the students and the environment within which they are serving. It was briefly mentioned that while residence life professional staff are responsible for designing and implementing RA training programs, they are often asked to do so without any formal training in teaching or curriculum design (Koch, 2016). There are several steps housing and residence life departments can take to improve the training experience for both professional staff and the participating students. First, departments can offer opportunities to gain experience in teaching and curriculum design through professional development funding; this means setting funds aside each year dedicated to staff training in these areas. Second, departments can encourage their employees to enroll in courses related to teaching and learning or curriculum design using a tuition benefit (if applicable). This may mean being flexible with work schedules if their classes are during work hours, but the benefits of staff development in these areas outweigh the temporary inconvenience of rearranging shifts.

Another option is to require training in these areas as part of the onboarding process for new hires and as part of yearly continuing education for current employees. In addition, tapping into the experts and resources within an institution may yield opportunities for excellent training from faculty, teaching and learning staff, and experts in the fields of teaching and curriculum design—and at a minimal cost to the department. Developing partnerships with other departments on campus, as well as specific staff and faculty, could lead to long-term programming for housing and residence life staff without the expense of travel and registration for an outside conference or training.

Supervision

Quality supervision can help increase employee retention and job satisfaction; this applies to full-time, professional staff as well as student employees (Berg & Brown, 2019). Research suggests that employing supervision that focuses on both departmental goals and employee development leads to lower levels of role ambiguity in the RA position (Berg & Brown, 2019). Lower levels of ambiguity are associated with greater job satisfaction among RAs (Brecheisen, 2015), which suggests supervision may play a role in RAs understanding their position as well as feeling satisfied performing the role.

Results of the ISPL-US demonstrate that RAs received regular feedback and that most often, this came from the person serving as their supervisor. Further, RAs had opportunities to regularly reflect on this feedback, and to debrief with their supervisor, other RAs, and through writing and reflection exercises. While the specific style of supervision received is not known, there appears to be a focus on both the personal and professional development of the RAs, which is associated with positive outcomes (Brecheisen, 2015). Continuing this process of regular communication, a focus on personal and professional development, and providing constructive feedback, and the opportunity to reflect on and learn from it, appear vital to establishing a meaningful supervisory relationship for all involved.

The Well-Being of Resident Assistants

While not explicitly asked through the ISPL-US, readers can make inferences regarding the well-being of students serving as RAs. Indicators such as feelings of belonging and welcome, contributing to their community, and ability to build relationships, each saw increases. A sense of belonging is protective of mental health in college students (Gopalan & Brady, 2019), which means it is associated with a lower likelihood of negative mental health outcomes and may reduce the impact of other risk factors when present. However, research has also found that students from minoritized identities, specifically students who hold underrepresented racial and ethnic identities, first-generation students, and low-income students, report a lower sense of belonging compared to their peers (Gopalan & Brady, 2019). While sense of belonging is an important indicator of mental health, it is also one that appears to vary based on identity. Consequently, understanding that each RA experiences belonging differently is significant. If leaders make consistent efforts to create inclusive and welcoming spaces for all students, they are more likely to be able to offer belonging to all students on their campus.

Career Readiness and Employability

The National Association of Colleges and Employers (NACE; 2023) defines career readiness as "a foundation from which to demonstrate requisite core competencies that broadly prepare the college educated for success in the workplace and lifelong career management" (para. 1). NACE (2023) has identified and defined eight career readiness competencies: career and self-development, communication, critical thinking, equity and inclusion, leadership, professionalism, teamwork, and technology. ISPL-US results demonstrate growth in each of these eight core competencies through the RA peer leadership experience. For example, students identified several types of communication skills that had increased, including interpersonal and written communication skills, presentation skills, the ability to share items in writing, and providing direction through interpersonal persuasion. These skills could be mapped to the NACE competencies of communication, leadership, and professionalism. Further, the skills of leadership, adaptability, creativity, problem solving, decision making, creating innovative approaches to complete a task, bringing together information learned from different places, and applying knowledge to real world settings through hands on experiences, could be mapped to the NACE competency of critical thinking. Students who served as RAs noted increases in their knowledge about, interactions with, and understanding of people with different backgrounds from their own, as well as in their ability to engage in ethical decision making; these could map to the NACE equity and inclusion competency.

The connection between RA skills and NACE (2023) competencies indicates that serving as an RA provides students with the opportunity to develop skills that translate into future employment and leadership positions. Understanding which skills and competencies translate into future employment for RAs enables housing and residence life departments to thoughtfully design the RA experience. Similar to identifying competencies and learning outcomes for a course, housing and residence life staff could design the RA experience to lead to the achievement of specific skills and outcomes at its completion. This could be achieved by mapping specific trainings and job responsibilities to the competencies, and identifying the skills that are developed through those experiences. These skills and competencies could also be used as a checkpoint to ensure that students serving as RAs are on track to leave the position with tangible growth in key areas that will serve them in their future endeavors.

Formal and informal evaluations regarding these skills and competency areas could be incorporated for a tangible measure of the growth over the course of their time in the RA position. A self-assessment, similar to that used in the ISPL-US, would allow RAs to rate their skills; this could be done at intervals to allow for an assessment of change over time. For example, this could be completed during RA onboarding or initial training (e.g., at baseline), at key milestones such as halfway through their contract or at the middle or end of a term, and at the end of their contract or time in the role. This information would not only assist RAs in assesing their own growth and development, but would also provide feedback for departments in assessing the effectiveness of their trainings, supervision, and staff performance. A comprehensive set of questions assessing aspects of the RA role has been developed and tested by Manata et al. (2017) with promising results; utilizing this question set, or others, can further their refinement as tools and provide additional evidence for their reliability and validity.

Diverse Identities and the RA Experience

Results from the ISPL-US indicate diverse representation among RAs. More than one in four was a first-generation student, and just shy of 30% were Pell Grant eligible (e.g., low-income). Almost one in 10 (7.7%) identified as non-binary, while one in three identified as being from a minority racial or ethnic group (e.g., a racial/ethnic group other than White). Diverse representation among students serving as RAs means that residents will interact with both peers and leaders with whom they can identify. Being part of identity-affirming environments can lead to growth and development among all students, including those from minoritized groups (Schuster, 2023); while exposure to individuals with differing backgrounds positively affects graduation and retention rates and engages students in a process of learning that offers deeper insight into self and appreciation for people who are different than themselves (Kuh et al., 2010). Consciously creating diverse and identity-affirming environments must be a focus of residence life staff. Institutions should regularly review departmental policies and procedures, from the marketing, recruitment, and hiring of RAs, to supervision and training, and student programming. This review process should also focus on seeking out best practices for these areas, and then implementing them. Collecting demographic data from RAs—or requesting it through an institution's institutional research office—can position leaders to better understand who does and does not have access to the RA experience.

Compensation

Compensation for RAs must also be a part of any conversation regarding access and equity in the higher education and residence life arenas. Seven in 10 students reported that earning an income while studying was a motivator for becoming an RA (70.2%), while 59.1% reported that they became an RA at least in part to have reduced study or accommodation fees. However, more than one in five students received no compensation for their work as an RA—meaning they did not receive pay (e.g., stipend, hourly wage), room, board, grant, scholarship, or any other financial renumeration for their work in what has been identified as a critical role on campus (e.g., Correa et al., 2023; Hernandez & Smith, 2019). While students serving as RAs will undoubtedly receive rewards through their personal and professional growth (Boone, 2018), this alone is not enough.

Not compensating RAs monetarily has negative implications for students who simply cannot afford to invest the time in being an RA without pay. If institutions are committed to access and equity and attracting students of all identities and backgrounds to serve in the RA role, fair compensation must be a priority. How an institution defines "fair" will vary, as there is no standardized job description for an RA. Ultimately, the requirements vary from campus to campus, leaving room for compensation to vary as well. However, reviewing RA compensation and determining a fair package based on specific job requirements and responsibilities is critical. At a minimum, institutions must be transparent about the compensation package for RAs in all communication regarding the position. If an institution does not currently compensate their RAs or wishes to engage in a good faith conversation about increasing the compensation package, it may take creativity to accomplish this. This may involve a partnership with the financial aid office to offer a grant or another way to offset costs, for example, if the position is eligible for work study. This would allow campuses to offset hourly pay for eligible students through federal funding, and place less of a financial burden on the department. Rather than RAs being "utility players," the role could be more specialized. With a specific focus area, this could translate into fewer hours worked per student and open the opportunity for additional paid work through other roles on or off campus.

Directions for Future Research

The responsibilities of the RA position continue to grow and are increasingly complex. These changes have led to rising levels of stress and burnout among students. This begs an integral question: What are the essential functions of the RA position? While there may be a way to standardize the position description for RAs, it is likely that institutions may still find nuance in how the role functions on their campus. A retrospective look at prior ISPL-US findings related to RAs may provide insight into whether and how student experiences within the role have changed over time. Are students as satisfied with their experience as an RA now as in years prior? Have the skills they identified developing through their RA experiences changed? Have the demographics of the students serving as RAs shifted? These are examples of the unanswered questions that researchers might explore by comparing these findings with prior ISPL results.

As mentioned earlier, ACUHO-I has a data benchmarking tool called the Campus Housing Index (CHI; 2023b). Since 2016, the CHI has collected data from housing and residence life staff about their institutions, including RA responsibilities and compensation. Participation in the CHI will help bolster knowledge of the position and how it functions across institutions. Utilizing CHI data to supplement that provided by the ISPL-US will serve to provide a more holistic view. Continued participation in both, by as many institutions as possible, will ensure the most reliable and accurate data are available.

Case Study: Rethinking the RA Role

Weighing the benefits and negative outcomes students serving as RAs experience has led to a discussion of whether the RA role, responsibilities, and function within the residence life department should adapt. From eliminating the position entirely, to overhauling the expectations, to making no changes, opinions regarding best practices vary. I have provided the following case study to help illustrate one approach to revising the RA position.

George Washington University

George Washington University (GWU) has become a trailblazer in the movement to rethink the RA role and how it functions on college and university campuses. During the pandemic, GWU took time to review the position and its responsibilities and make changes, with a goal of improving the overall student experience. This process led to changes to not only their staffing model, but the structure of the residential environment on campus (GW Today, 2021, 2022). These changes included:

- Implementing a neighborhood concept with residence halls assigned to one of five neighborhoods (GW Today, 2022)

- Creating a new live-in professional staff position (Community Coordinator) assigned to each residential building (GW Today, 2022)

- Removing the crisis response responsibility from RAs and assigning it to Community Coordinators (GW Today, 2021; Johanson, 2023)

- Replacing the traditional RA role with four new student positions (Johanson, 2023)

  - Programming Assistant

  - Operations Assistant

  - Communications Assistant

  - Peer Mediator

- Continuing to hire students for three positions that existed prior to this change

  - Special Projects Assistant (three positions)

  - Main Office Assistant

  - Technology Assistant

With the change to nine positions, over 200 students are now employed (Johanson, 2023). Administrators updated the three pre-existing roles, and all nine positions now have specific learning objectives and expectations mapped to them (Johanson, 2023). These changes are meant to allow RAs to continue to serve in a PL capacity that provides deep meaning while developing a greater understanding of and expertise in their specific role (GW Today, 2021). By removing the crisis response aspect and reassigning it to professional staff, the University feels it is removing the main cause of stress and burnout among RAs, while also directly connecting students in crisis with trained professionals (Mangan, 2021).

GWU remains a trailblazer in its revisioning of the RA role. While other institutions may be starting to critically assess RA responsibilities, none yet have announced plans to change the position as considerably as GWU (Mangan, 2021). Can the RA peer leadership experience remain the same if the position, and its responsibilities, change so drastically? What is the impact of creating multiple, specialized RA positions on campus for both RAs and residents? Will RAs report less burnout and stress with crisis response responsibilities shifting to staff? There is much that is still unknown about these changes and their impact on students and peer leadership. However, GWU is in the unique position of serving as a case study for what might be the future of the RA position.

Conclusion

Results of the ISPL-US are clear: Serving as an RA leads to considerable growth in students. This unique PL experience gives students the opportunity to develop skills that prepare them for academic success, future employment, and considerable personal growth. RAs encounter a diversity of ideas, experiences, and individuals, leading to change in their worldview and greater engagement in their communities on and off campus. However, there is also growing evidence that, like other helping professions, RAs experience secondary trauma, burnout, and emotional turmoil through their work (Correa et al., 2023). The ISPL-US results also raised questions about equitable compensation for RAs, as more than one in five reported receiving no compensation. This has implications for recruiting and retaining RAs from minoritized backgrounds. The case study highlights one way of changing this unique PL role; however, whether and how this position should be reimagined, as well as how these changes impact the PL experience, warrant further study.

References

Association of College & University Housing Officers - International [ACUHO-I]. (2023a). *ACUHO-I Future of the Profession: Phase II Discovery Report.*

Association of College & University Housing Officers - International [ACUHO-I]. (2023b). *2022 Campus Housing Index report: The state of live-in staff: Graduate assistants, paraprofessionals, and professional staff.*

Berg, S. A., & Brown, C. G. (2019). An examination of the supervision and job satisfaction factors of residence directors and resident assistants. *Journal of College & University Student Housing, 46*(1), 30-45.

Boone, K. B. (2018). Resident assistant workplace motivation. *Journal of College & University Student Housing, 44*(2), 28-43.

Boone, K. B., Davidson, D. L., & Bauman, M. (2016). The evolution and increasing complexity of the resident assistant role in the United States from colonial to modern times. *Journal of College & University Student Housing, 42*(3), 38-51.

Brecheisen, S. M. (2015). Paraprofessional staff in transition: The sophomore RA experience. *Journal of College & University Student Housing, 42*(1), 194-211.

Correa, A. B., Pham, H., Bucklin, R., Sewell, D., & Afifi, R. (2023). Students supporting students: Evaluating the impact of the COVID-19 pandemic on resident assistant mental health. *Journal of American College Health, 71*, 1-11. https://doi.org/10.1080/07448481.2023.2201867

Fassett, K. T., Gonyea, R. M., Fosnacht, K., & Graham, P. A. (2021). *The case for campus housing: Results from a national study - A brief for housing and residence life professionals.* ACUHO-I. https://www.acuho-i.org/wp-content/uploads/2024/03/2024_caseforcampushousing_residencelife.pdf

Fosnacht, K., Gonyea, K. M., & Graham, P. A. (2020). The relationship of first-year residence hall roommate assignment policy with interactional diversity and perceptions of the campus environment. *Journal of Higher Education, 91*(5), 781-804. https://doi.org/10.1080/00221546.2019.1689483

Foste, Z., & Johnson, S. (2021). Diversity cupcakes and White institutional space: The emotional labor of Resident Assistants of Color at historically White institutions. *Journal of College Student Development, 62*(4), 389-404.

Gopalan, M., & Brady, S. T. (2019). College students' sense of belonging: A national perspective. *Educational Researcher, 49*(2), 134-137. https://doi.org/10.3102/0013189X19897622

Graham, P. A., Hurtado, S. S., & Gonyea, R. M. (2018). The benefits of living on campus: Do residence halls provide distinctive environments of engagement? *Journal of Student Affairs Research and Practice, 55*(3), 255-269. https://doi.org/10.1080/19496591.2018.1474752

GW Today. (2021, February 24). GW to transform service and care for residential students. https://gwtoday.gwu.edu/gw-transform-service-and-care-residential-students

GW Today. (2022, March 7). Reimagined residential professional staffing model celebrates early progress. https://gwtoday.gwu.edu/reimagined-residential-professional-staffing-model-celebrates-early-progress

Hernandez, C. L., & Smith, H. G. (2019). Leadership development in paraprofessional roles. *New Directions for Student Leadership, 2019*(162), 75-89. https://doi.org/10.1002/yd.20335

Johanson, C. (2023, June 26-29). *Engagement beyond the RA* [Conference session]. Campus Home. Live! 2023 ACUHO-I Conference & Expo, Portland, OR, United States.

Koch, V. A. (2016). Current practices in resident assistant training. *Journal of College & University Student Housing, 42*(3), 80-97.

Kuh, G. D., Kinzie, J., Schuh, J. H., & Whitt, E. J. (2010). *Student success in college: Creating conditions that matter.* Jossey-Bass.

Linley, J. L. (2018). Racism here, racism there, racism everywhere: The racial realities of minoritized peer socialization agents at a historically White institution. *Journal of College Student Development, 59*(1), 21-36. https://psycnet.apa.org/doi/10.1353/csd.2018.0002

Manata, B., DeAngelis, B. N., Paik, J. E., & Miller, V. D. (2017). Measuring critical aspects of the resident assistant role. *Journal of College Student Development, 58*(4), 618-623. https://doi.org/10.1353/csd.2017.0046

Mangan, K. (2021, February 25). Too much for students to handle? Why one university decided to do away with RAs. *The Chronicle of Higher Education.* https://www.chronicle.com/article/too-much-for-students-to-handle-why-one-university-decided-to-do-away-with-ras

Martin, G. L., & Blechschmidt, S. (2014). The impact of being a resident assistant on intercultural effectiveness and socially responsible leadership development during college. *Journal of College & University Student Housing, 40*(2), 30-45.

McClure, C., Birong, G., Anderson, J., Brunn, P., Jang, E. Y., & Krier-Jenkins, A. (2022). Understanding the impact of resident assistant experiences on their professional quality of life: The case for increased institutional supports. *Journal of College & University Student Housing, 48*(2), 70-93.

Mollett, A., Weaver, K. E., Holmes, J. M., Linley, J. L., Hurley, E., & Renn, K. A. (2021). Queer in residence: Exploring the on-campus housing exeriences of queer college students. *Journal of Student Affairs Research and Practice, 58*(1), 1-14. https://doi.org/10.1080/19496591.2020.1717962

National Association of Colleges and Employers (NACE). (2023, October 8). *What is career readiness?* https://www.naceweb.org/career-readiness/competencies/career-readiness-defined

Nelson Laird, T. F., Engberg, M. E., & Hurtado, S. (2005). Modeling accentuation effects: Enrolling in a diversity course and the importance of social action engagement. *The Journal of Higher Education, 76*(4), 448-476. https://doi.org/10.1080/00221546.2005.11772292

Schuster, M. T. (2023). Well-being and the experiences of resident assistants with minoritized identities. *Journal of College & University Student Housing, 49*(3), 126-145.

Schuster, M. T., & Stalker, R. (2022). Resident assistants with minoritized identities: The promise of identity-affirming micro-climates in enhancing RA experiences. *Journal of College & University Student Housing, 49*(1), 10-31.

Soria, K. M., & Roberts, B. J. (2023). The effect of serving as a resident assistant on undergraduates' prosocial behaviors. *Journal of Student Affairs Research and Practice, 60*(2), 236-249. https://doi.org/10.1080/19496591.2022.2041427

Strange, C. C., & Banning, J. H. (2015). *Designing for learning: Creating campus environments for student success.* John Wiley & Sons.

Walker, W. B. (2022). Let's rethink the role: A critical reflection addressing responsibilities of undergraduate resident assistants. *Journal of the Student Personnel Association at Indiana University,* 21-29.

Chapter 5

Peer Leadership in the First-Year Experience: A Pathway Toward Belonging

Bryce D. Bunting
Brigham Young University

Dallin George Young
University of Georgia

Peer leaders (PLs) play a crucial role in the first year by serving as relatable models, offering support and guidance as new students navigate new expectations and academic requirements, helping foster a sense of belonging, and helping their peers participate in their new community (Greenfield et al., 2013). Consequently, the use of PLs in the first-year experience (FYE) has continued to grow (e.g., Keup, 2020; van der Meer et al., 2022; Young et al., 2023). Indeed, slightly over one third (34.5%, $n = 477$) of the respondents to the U.S. administration of the International Survey of Peer Leaders (ISPL-US) indicated that they were working in a first-year context.

We have defined an FYE PL as one whose work is focused on offering support, guidance, or mentoring specifically to new students, including transfer students, from the time of their admission through to the end of their first year on campus. (Note: this did not include PLs in orientation roles; see Chapter 3 for results related to students in orientation leader roles.) The questions that guided our analysis of the ISPL-US data included:

- What kinds of experiences do FYE PLs report having? What are they learning? What skills are they developing?

- How does FYE peer leadership strengthen PLs' sense of belonging on their campus?

- How do the structural elements of the experience FYE PL experience align with the characteristics of high-impact practices (HIPs)?

As with the other PL roles discussed in this volume, FYE PLs experienced significant growth. We also discovered in our early analyses that these PLs reported significantly greater levels of satisfaction with their experience than did the overall survey sample. Consequently, we began to wonder if there may have been meaningful differences in the structure of the experiences of FYE PLs. And, as we introduced in Chapter 2, we were curious about how the three modes of transition—community, participation, and becoming—might be apparent in various elements of the PL role.

In the remainder of this chapter, we will discuss (a) how FYE PLs report or describe their experiences, (b) how the experiences of FYE PLs seems to differ from the experiences of PLs in contexts outside the first year of college, and (c) how FYE peer leadership might serve as a HIP and contribute to a sense of belonging for those who serve as PLs. We will conclude by sharing implications for practice and then discussing avenues for future research.

What Did First-Year Experience Peer Leaders Report About Their Experience?

We have broken this discussion into three subsections: (a) a brief demographic profile of FYE PLs, (b) discussion of what FYE PLs reported about the structure of their experience, and (c) what FYE PLs reported relative to key learning and institutional outcomes. By highlighting data regarding the structure and learning of FYE PLs, we can explore how the structural elements of the peer leadership experience might influence what PLs learn and how they grow through their work.

Demographics

We first wanted to better understand who reported having served in an FYE PL role, particularly whether there were certain demographic groups who were under or overrepresented in this segment of the survey sample. In general, there were no significant differences in participation as an FYE PL relative to gender, age, or class standing. However, we did observe interesting patterns relative to FYE PLs' reported socioeconomic status, as well as their race and ethnicity.

Among FYE PLs, 39.3% reported that they were Pell eligible, 32.5% reported that they were not Pell eligible, and 32.1% were unsure of their eligibility for Pell Grant funding. The results of a chi-square test of independence demonstrated that FYE PLs were significantly more likely to have reported being Pell-eligible than were the rest of the PLs in the sample, $X2$ $(2, n = 1378) = 6.32$, $p = .042$. In most cases, there was no relationship between being an FYE PL and students' race and ethnicity; however, there were two exceptions. First, Asian or Asian American respondents were less likely to report being FYE PLs, with 24.6% of Asian/Asian-American respondents reporting work as an FYE PL, compared to 35.4% across all other categories of race and ethnicity, $X2$ $(1, n = 1379) = 5.64$, $p = .018$. Second, Hispanic and Latino/a PLs were more likely to report having worked in an FYE setting, with 43.3% of Latino/a PLs reporting involvement in an FYE PL role, compared to 33.0% in all other race and ethnicity categories, $X2$ $(1, n = 1379) = 6.32$, $p = .004$.

The data collected through the ISPL-US do not provide much clarity on why PLs with financial need are more likely to have served as FYE PLs. Our initial hypothesis was that FYE PL roles might be more likely to include financial compensation; however, the results of a chi-square test of independence (see Table 5.4 later in this chapter) showed that FYE PLs were no more or less likely to have received financial compensation for their work. As we will discuss throughout this chapter, serving as an FYE PL seems to function as a pathway to a sense of belonging for PLs. Consequently, future research should be conducted to better understand how students' identities might influence their decisions to become an FYE PL.

Key Structural Elements of the FYE Peer Leadership Experience

We observed three noteworthy patterns in the structure of the FYE PL experience: initial and ongoing training, opportunities to receive feedback, and forms of compensation. Each of these elements impacts the learning that PLs experience. Additionally, these are all simple things for institutional leaders to modify to enhance PL learning. Consequently, we feel they are fruitful spaces for reflection, evaluation, and adaptation on campuses where there is interest in enhancing the benefits of being a PL.

Training

Providing well-designed training is critical to helping PLs fulfill their responsibilities and experience personal growth. Additionally, an investment in the learning and development of PLs aligns with our earlier discussions around the value of prioritizing becoming in student transitions. As shown in Figure 5.1, the vast majority of the FYE PLs participating in the ISPL-US (95.3%) reported receiving initial training for all or most of the PL positions they held, which is slightly higher than the overall percentage of PLs in the sample who reported receiving initial training for all or most of their PL roles (87.2%). In general, FYE PLs begin their experience with at least some basic knowledge and skill for their role. Additionally, it appears that for most FYE PLs, this initial training is in-depth, lasting one week or longer (see Figure 5.2).

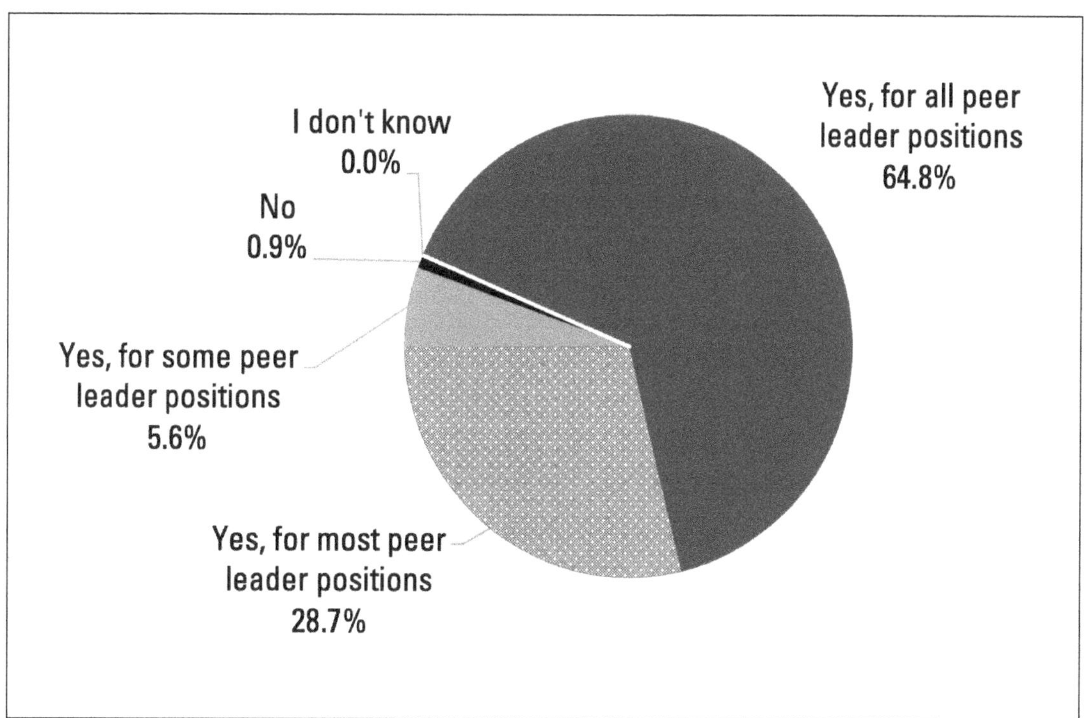

Figure 5.1 Initial Training among Students in FYE PL Roles. (*n* = 457)

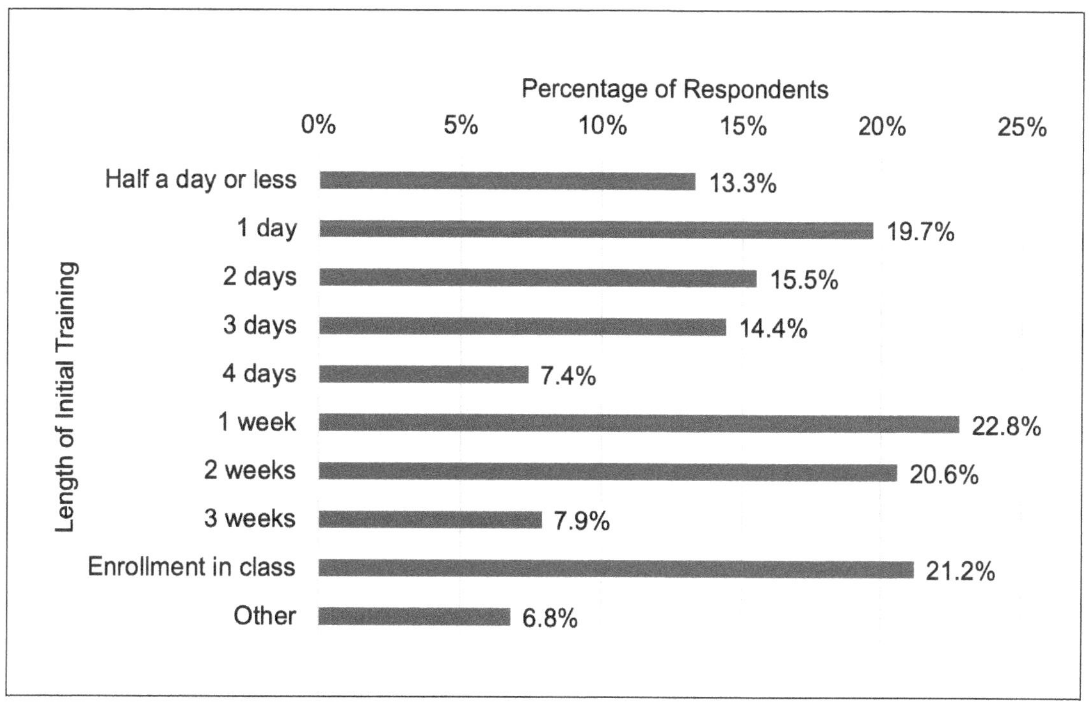

Figure 5.2 Length of Initial Training for Students in FYE PL Roles (*n* = 457)
Note. Students could report more than one length; therefore, the sum of percentages will be greater than 100%.

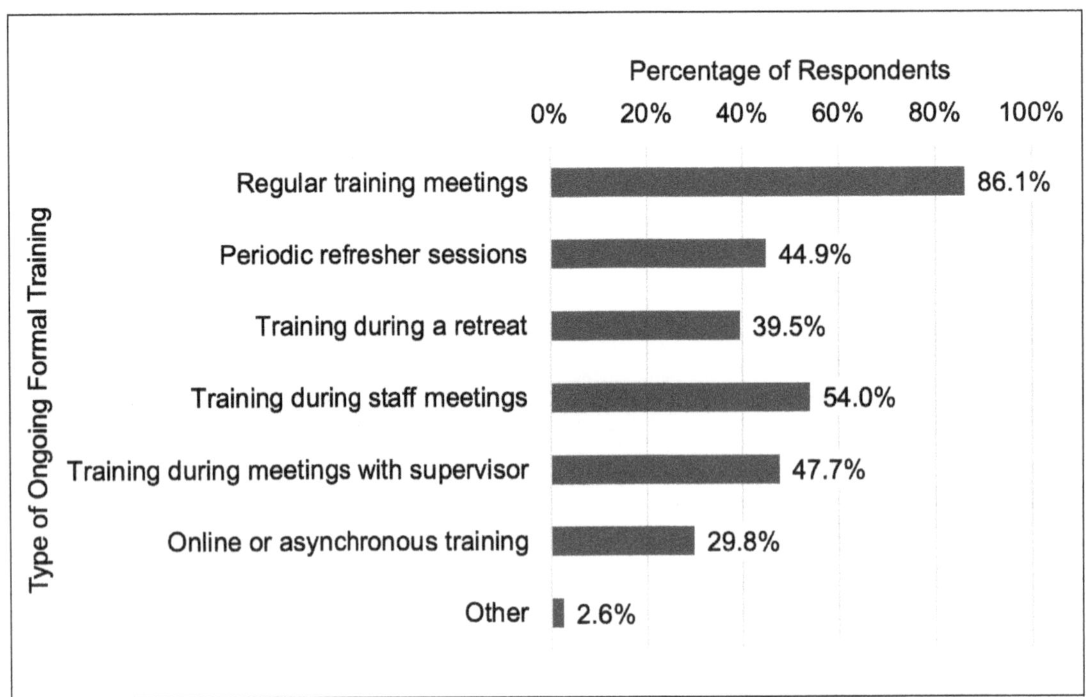

Figure 5.3 Types of Ongoing Training Reported by Students in FYE PL Roles (*n* = 352)

Note. Students could report more than one type of training; therefore, the sum of percentages will be greater than 100%.

While the vast majority of FYE PLs in the sample reported receiving some kind of initial training for all or most of their PL positions, a smaller percentage of this group (77.5%) reported that they received ongoing training in their PL positions. The most common channels of delivery were (a) regular or ongoing meetings dedicated specifically to training (86.1%), (b) training delivered during general staff meetings (54.0%), and (c) training provided during meetings with a supervisor (47.7%; see Figure 5.3).

As was the case for initial training, FYE PLs were slightly more likely to have reported receiving ongoing training than were survey respondents in general (73.7%); nevertheless, there is room for improvement when it comes to providing FYE PLs with supplemental training beyond what is provided at the outset of their experience. Extending training beyond the onboarding process and across the PL experience increases the potential for PLs to experience meaningful personal becoming.

Feedback on Performance

One of the key characteristics of HIPs is frequent, timely, and constructive feedback (Kuh & O'Donnell, 2013); feedback is also an additional way of contributing to becoming among PLs. While the ISPL did not facilitate evaluation of the quality of the feedback PLs were receiving, it did provide insight into how often PLs had "regular" opportunities to receive performance feedback. Among FYE PLs in the survey, 74.5% reported regular opportunities for feedback. This feedback was most often delivered through meetings with supervising faculty or staff members (79.8%; see Figure 5.4).

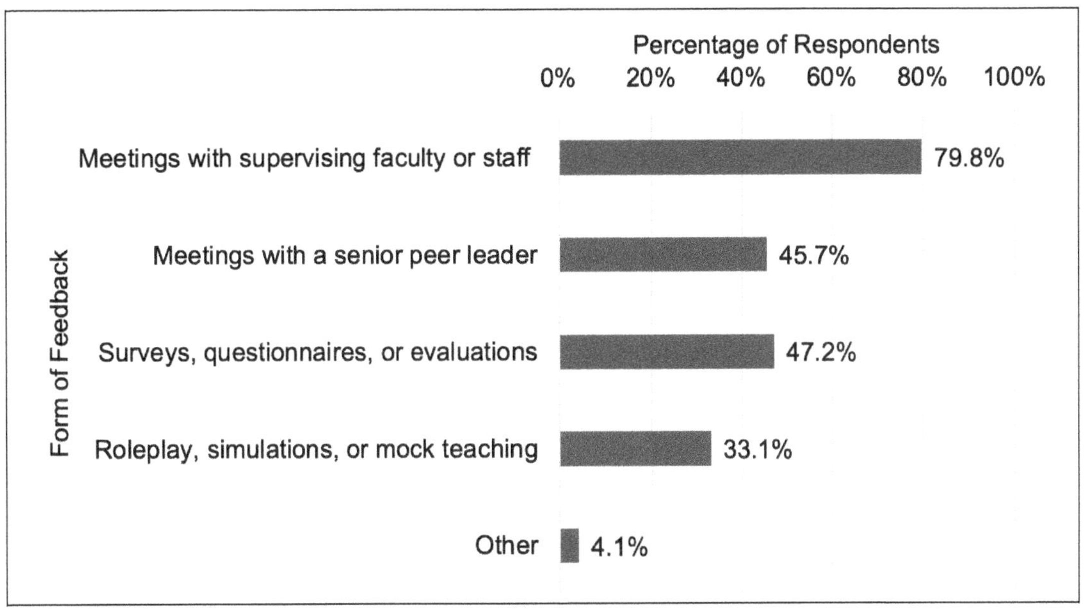

Figure 5.4 How Students in FYE PL Roles Received Feedback on their Performance (*n* = 341)

Note. Students could report more than one form of feedback; therefore, the sum of percentages will be greater than 100%.

Compensation

As is seen in Figure 5.5, approximately two thirds of the FYE PLs in the ISPL-US reported receiving compensation. By far, the most common compensation for both FYE PLs (80.2%) and the broader ISPL-US sample (78.2%) was an hourly wage or stipend. Just over one fifth of FYE PLs reported receiving course credit for their work. We also feel it important to highlight the fact that over one third of FYE PLs (36.8%) reported that at least one of their PL roles was voluntary (slightly higher than the overall sample, 34.3%). This concerns us given what it may mean for access, equity, and inclusion. We will discuss this in more depth later in the report.

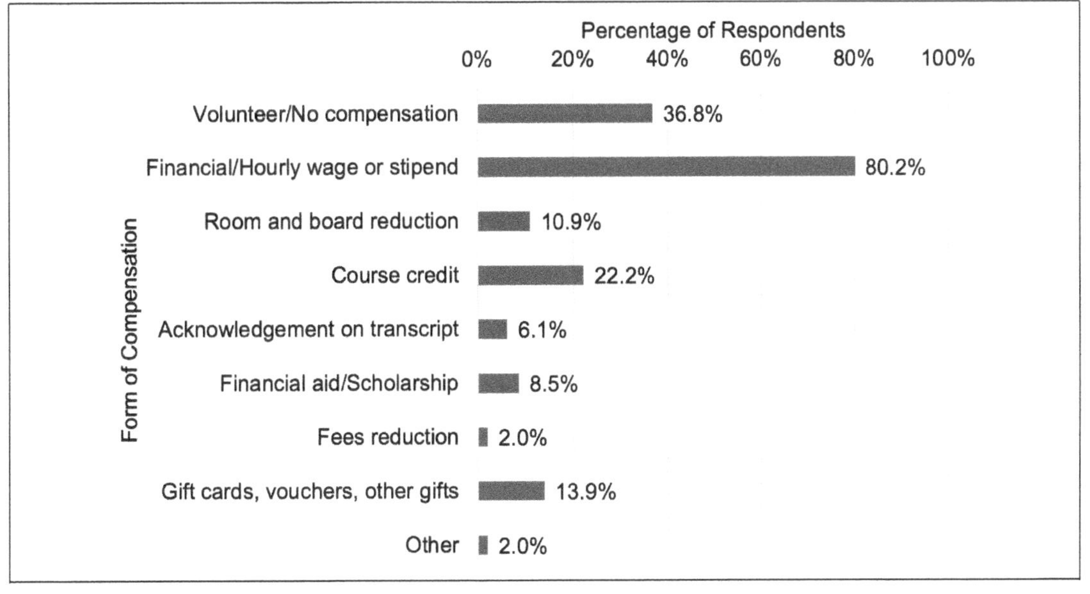

Figure 5.5 Forms of Compensation for Students in FYE PL Roles (*n* = 459)

Note. Students could report more than one form of compensation; therefore, the sum of percentages will be greater than 100%.

Key Learning and Institutional Outcomes Among First-Year Peer Leaders

We have focused this section of the chapter on FYE PLs' learning and growth in two domains: (a) academic skill development and employability, and (b) sense of institutional connection and belonging, and have focused our discussion on these outcomes due to increasing calls for accountability in these areas and the continual need to demonstrate higher education's impact on student learning and future career competence.

Academic Skill Development and Employability

Across nearly every skill domain, FYE PLs reported some degree of gain or development associated with their PL experience. As illustrated in Table 5.1, academic skill development gains were greatest for creativity, time management, critical thinking, interpersonal communication, problem solving, and decision-making. The most notable growth in 21st century learning and employability outcomes related to building relationships with other PLs and applying knowledge to real-life settings through hands-on experiences (see Table 5.2). These data seem to indicate that when thoughtfully designed the FYE PL experience attends to all three modes of transition by facilitating the development of meaningful community relationships, offering opportunities for participation in authentic real-world activities, and fostering learning and becoming.

Institutional Connection and Belonging

The most pronounced gains reported by FYE PLs related to their feelings of connection to their institution, interactions with members of the campus community, and feelings of belonging (see Table 5.3). Serving as an FYE PL was also associated with notable increases in students' interaction with people with backgrounds different than their own, their desire to stay at their institution and graduate, and feelings of contributing to the campus community. Thus, serving as an FYE PL seems to provide a particularly powerful pathway toward connection, community, and sense of belonging for students who serve in these roles.

Table 5.1

Increase in Academic Skills Among Students in FYE PL Roles

Skills	***n***	***M***	***SD***
Academic	444	5.17	1.18
Presentation	451	5.88	0.96
Problem solving	444	6.09	0.99
Decision making	447	6.05	0.97
Adaptability	446	5.89	1.00
Creativity	445	6.41	0.79
Critical thinking	448	6.18	0.88
Time management	448	6.27	0.88
Organizational	450	5.50	1.10
Project management	446	5.85	1.07
Leadership	450	5.89	1.00
Teamwork and collaboration	446	5.83	1.02
Interpersonal communication	451	6.18	0.93
Written communication	451	5.74	1.01

Note. Participants were asked to rate their agreement with the statement that their academic skills had changed as a result of their PL experiences on a seven-point scale from "greatly decreased" (1) to "greatly increased" (7).

Table 5.2

Increase in 21st Century Learning Outcomes Among Students in FYE PL Role

21st Century Learning Outcome	n	M	SD
Analyzing a problem from new perspectives	448	5.81	0.97
Creating innovative approaches to complete a task	448	5.71	1.01
Providing direction through interpersonal persuasion	429	5.75	0.99
Sharing ideas with others in writing	444	5.42	1.11
Building relationships with people with whom you work	450	6.20	0.87
Engaging in ethical decision	443	5.74	1.07
Bringing together information learned from different places	443	5.98	0.97
Applying knowledge to real-world settings	444	6.04	0.99
Succeeding in a full-time job after graduation	375	5.58	1.13

Note. Participants were asked to rate their agreement with the statement that their academic skills had changed as a result of their PL experiences on a seven-point scale from "greatly decreased" (1) to "greatly increased" (7).

Table 5.3

Reported Increase in Institutional Connection and Belonging for Students in FYE PL Role

Skills	n	M	SD
Meaningful interaction with faculty	453	5.72	1.13
Desire to engage in continuous learning following graduation	451	5.97	1.00
Feeling that you are contributing to your campus community	447	6.25	0.87
Meaningful interaction with staff	448	6.11	0.92
Meaningful interaction with peers	451	6.12	0.92
Knowledge about people with backgrounds different than yours	448	6.09	0.92
Interaction with people with backgrounds different than yours	447	6.59	0.69
Understanding of people with backgrounds different than yours	446	6.06	1.09
Knowledge of campus resources	451	5.85	1.21
Feeling that you belong and are welcome at your institution	448	5.79	1.19
Your desire to graduate from your	452	6.30	0.84

Note. Participants were asked to rate their agreement with the statement that their institutional connection outcomes had increased as a result of their PL experiences on a seven-point scale of agreement from "greatly increased" (1) to "greatly decreased" (7).

How was the Experience of First-Year Experience Peer Leaders Unique?

One of the final items of the ISPL invited participants to indicate their general level of satisfaction with all their PL experiences using a seven-point Likert scale (1 = "very dissatisfied," 4 = "neutral," 7 = "very satisfied"). Across the entire sample of ISPL-US participants, the mean rating for this item was 6.13 (n = 1273, SD = 1.03), indicating that regardless of the particular PL role played students are satisfied with their experiences.

Given this high level of overall satisfaction across the ISPL-US sample, we were surprised to find that FYE PLs reported an even higher level of satisfaction (6.29, SD = 0.88, n = 450) than did PLs in other roles

(6.04, SD = 1.09, *n* = 823). Further, the results of an independent-samples t-test indicated that the difference in these two means was highly significant (t(1271) = 4.15, p < .001). Consequently, we began to wonder what might have contributed to FYE PLs' particularly high levels of satisfaction. Our hope was that by looking more closely at the structure of the FYE PL experience, we might be able to identify structural elements that could be incorporated into any PL experience.

Again, we observed notable differences in the ways FYE PLs were reporting on their experiences across two domains: (a) training, supervision, and compensation and (b) institutional connection and belonging. Based on these observations and our hypothesis that there may be subtle, yet significant, structural differences in the experiences of FYE PLs and PLs in other roles, we conducted chi-square tests of independence to test these assumptions.

Training, Supervision, and Compensation

Because training, supervision, and compensation are all elements of the PL experience that can be adjusted, we were interested in exploring the differences in these structural elements between FYE PLs and PLs in other roles. The results of a chi-square test of independence focused on these features of the PL experience are provided in Table 5.4.

As outlined in Table 5.4, FYE PLs were significantly more likely than PLs in other role types to report having received some degree of both initial (p < .001) and ongoing (p = .035) training. Additionally, FYE PLs were significantly more likely to have reported receiving regular opportunities to reflect on what they were learning in their role (p = .013). Thus, there were key differences in the training and supervision received by FYE PLs that aligned with the characteristics of HIPs identified by Kuh and O'Donnell (2013) and that opened the door for becoming (Young & Bunting, 2024). First, the opportunity to participate in in-depth and ongoing training represents a significant investment of time and energy on the part of FYE PLs. Second, by regularly reflecting on their learning, FYE PLs could integrate and apply their learning in powerful ways, as well as gain insight into how they were growing and changing. As is argued in other chapters in this report, this combination of focused training and regular reflection on experience is one of the most important ways of fostering learning and becoming among PLs.

The data in Table 5.4 also reveal interesting differences related to the way institutions compensate FYE PLs. Most notably, FYE PLs were much more likely to have received academic credit as part of their compensation. In previous research, Young and Keup (2018) found that receiving academic course credit was the most impactful form of compensation for the learning outcomes associated with peer leadership. They found that PLs who received course credit reported greater outcomes across several measures, including academic skill development; interactions with faculty, staff, and peers; academic commitment; employability outcomes; and traditional academic performance than PLs who were either volunteers or who received financial compensation.

We suggest that because FYE PLs were more likely to be in a credit-bearing course, they were also more likely to engage in the practices that enhanced their learning, including ongoing training for their role, meaningful interactions with faculty and peers, and regular reflection on and integration of their learning. Moreover, because they were having these meaningful educational experiences and experiencing meaningful personal growth, it should be no surprise that they were highly satisfied with their time in PL roles.

Table 5.4

Comparisons of Training, Supervision, and Compensation by Participation in FYE PL Roles

Feature of PL experience	Students in FYE PL roles		Students not in FYE PL roles		x^2	p
	n	%	n	%		
Training and supervision						
Received some initial training[a]	459	99.1	831	94.9	15.69	< .001
Received ongoing training	354	77.5	593	71.5	6.68	.035
Provided with regular feedback[a]	342	74.5	652	74.9	0.02	.890
Provided with regular opportunities to reflect on learning	350	76.3	621	71.5	8.66	.013
Compensation						
Volunteer	169	36.8	286	33.0	1.92	.166
Financial	368	80.2	668	77.1	1.62	.203
Room and board	50	10.9	179	20.7	20.06	< .001
Course credit	102	22.2	124	14.3	13.25	< .001
Acknowledgement on transcript	28	6.1	55	6.4	0.03	.858
Financial aid	39	8.5	58	6.7	1.43	.232
Reduced fees	9	2.0	24	2.8	0.81	.368
Gift cards/vouchers	64	13.9	41	4.7	34.87	< .001

Note. This table presents the frequency and percentage of PLs' affirmative responses indicating the presence of training, supervision, or compensation in their experience.

[a] Responses to questions on initial training and feedback were collapsed into binary categories. All responses indicating "yes" were included in one category while responses indicating "no" and "I don't know" were included in the other.

Institutional Connection and Belonging

As is seen in Table 5.5, FYE PLs reported significantly higher degrees of connection, belonging, and experiences with peers whose backgrounds were different from their own. These differences in experience were especially pronounced for FYE PLs' interactions with staff and peers, knowledge of campus resources, desire to stay at their institution and graduate, feelings of contribution to the campus community, and knowledge of people with backgrounds different from their own.

We find these outcomes to be particularly noteworthy given the impact of students' sense of belonging on their overall experience. Simply put, few elements of the college experience have more of an impact on both students' success in and satisfaction with college than their feelings of community, support, membership, and acceptance on their campus (e.g., Gopalan & Brady, 2020; Nunn, 2021; Strayhorn, 2019). Consequently, the fact that FYE PLs report such high degrees of community, connection, and contribution, suggests that examination of the unique characteristics of FYE peer leadership can provide insight into how to enhance the experiences of PLs in other roles.

Table 5.5

Outcomes Related to Connection, Belonging, and Experience with Difference Compared by Participation in FYE PL Roles

Outcome	Students in FYE PL roles		Students not in FYE PL roles		t	p
	M	*SD*	*M*	*SD*		
Institutional connection and belonging						
Meaningful interaction with faculty	5.74	1.14	5.60	1.19	2.10	.036
Meaningful interaction with staff	5.99	1.02	5.79	1.11	3.20	.001
Meaningful interaction with peers	6.26	0.87	6.08	0.96	3.29	.001
Knowledge of campus resources	6.60	0.70	6.32	0.87	6.35	< .001
Feeling that you belong and are welcome at your institution	6.08	1.10	5.77	1.20	6.04	< .001
Desire to stay graduate from institution	5.86	1.21	5.53	1.35	4.53	< .001
Feeling of contributing to campus community	6.32	0.85	6.10	1.03	4.13	< .001
Ability to build relationships with colleagues	6.20	0.87	6.08	0.95	2.34	.019
Experiences with difference						
Knowledge about people with different backgrounds	6.12	0.93	5.94	1.06	3.27	.001
Interaction with people with different backgrounds	6.13	0.93	5.99	1.03	2.41	.016
Understanding of people with different backgrounds	6.11	0.93	5.95	1.02	2.78	.005

Note. Participants were asked to rate their agreement with the statement that selected outcomes had increased as a result of their PL experiences on a seven-point scale of agreement from "greatly increased" (1) to "greatly decreased" (7).

Insights from First-Year Experience Peer Leadership for Making Peer Leadership a High-Impact Practice and a Pathway to Belonging for All Peer Leaders

We hope that our discussion thus far in this chapter has demonstrated that there is much to be learned from the experiences of FYE PLs about how PL experiences can be designed and implemented to more fully leverage the potential for peer leadership to lead to belonging and transformative learning for the students who institutions employ in these roles. As we asserted in Chapter 1, under particular conditions, peer leadership holds a "triple-impact" in that it offers significant benefits to the students served, the PLs who provide this support, and to the institutions who administer these programs. However, to return to one of the overarching themes of this report, for any educational practice to yield the desired outcomes, it must be thoughtfully designed and grounded in empirically validated best practices.

We argue that the experiences reported by students in FYE PL roles in the ISPL-US were impactful precisely because they align with several of the characteristics of HIPs. Specifically, FYE PLs in the ISPL-US report significant gains related to various academic skills, including problem solving, creativity, critical thinking, time management, and interpersonal communication. Additionally, FYE PLs report significant outcomes related to various employability measures, such as building meaningful relationships with other PLs and applying knowledge in real-world settings. Most importantly, students in FYE PL roles report that their experiences align with many of the characteristics of HIPs (Kuh & O'Donnell, 2013) in that they:

- require a significant investment of time and energy; involve meaningful interactions with faculty and peers;

- provide regular interactions with people and circumstances that differ from those with which FYE PLs are familiar;

- offer frequent, timely, and constructive feedback;

- include periodic, structured opportunities to reflect and integrate their learning; and

- facilitate opportunities to apply their learning in real-world settings.

Because of these structural features, FYE PLs are not only learning a great deal in their role, but they are reporting a sense of belonging and connection to their institutions that is unique across the various PL roles that were included in the ISPL-US. Consequently, we assert that serving as a PL, especially in FYE contexts, provides students with a powerful way of participating in their institutional community, feeling genuine membership in this community, and developing a sense of connection to their institution that makes them significantly more likely to report a desire to persist to graduation.

Additionally, our analysis of the FYE PL data from the ISPL-US revealed alignment with the modes of transition introduced in Chapter 2 of this report—community, participation, and becoming (Young & Bunting, 2024). Like the characteristics of HIPs, these modes help to describe the characteristics of learning environments that not only provide support for students as they navigate common college transitions, but that leverage the potential of the college experience to contribute to deep and long-lasting learning that extends far beyond graduation. Though becoming a PL is not normally viewed as a college transition in the formal sense, students who step into these leadership roles are very much experiencing a transition. Indeed, taking on the role of a PL involves familiarizing oneself with new norms and policies, developing new skills, and becoming a different type of college student: one who understands the core purposes of higher education and what is required for success. Thus, it follows that peer leadership roles that intentionally leverage community, participation, and becoming are more likely to foster highly impactful learning.

These three modes are evident in the experiences reported by FYE PLs in our sample. First, they reported experiencing a high degree of community as evidenced by their meaningful interactions with faculty, staff, and peers; regular interactions with people whose backgrounds differ from their own; and opportunities to build relationships with the people with whom they worked (see Tables 5.4 and 5.5). A strong psychological sense of community (Schreiner et al., 2020) was also evident in FYE PLs' high levels of reported feelings of belonging and intentions to persist to graduation at their institution. Second, FYE PLs reported that their experiences offered meaningful opportunities to participate in and contribute to the work of their institution. Additionally, they reported that their experience offered regular opportunities for reflection on and application of what they were learning in their role.

Finally, the fact that FYE PLs were significantly more likely to report a desire to engage in continuous learning after graduating, and to report increases in various skills and abilities, suggests that their peer leadership experiences were critical factors in helping them move beyond simply occupying a position of "student" and to truly become "learners." Sanders (2018) has described this shift from externally motivated student to internally motivated and lifelong learner as the most important purpose of college.

Structuring PL learning environments in ways that provide access to community, participation, and becoming fosters learning experiences with transformative potential. We argue that when PLs are experiencing this kind of meaningful growth in their work and have opportunities to reflect on and articulate this learning, they are much more likely to report satisfaction with their experiences. Additionally, the opportunity to actively participate in the core work of the institution, by supporting the learning of their peers, serves as a powerful pathway toward the sense of community and belonging that are associated with so many other positive college outcomes (see Gopalan & Brady, 2020; Nunn, 2021; Strayhorn, 2019). This includes key metrics associated with retention, persistence, and post-graduation employability outcomes that serve as accountability measures on every college campus in America.

Implications and Practical Recommendations

While we have grounded the analysis and discussion in this chapter in the experiences of FYE PLs, our broader goal has been to use the experiences of this segment of the ISPL-US participants to elucidate the key characteristics of transformative and high-impact peer leadership environments that can inform practice and future research. By understanding these elements of experience and then prioritizing them in the design and implementation of peer leadership, institutions can be more intentional in facilitating experiences for student leaders that are truly educative. Additionally, by identifying these critical elements of PL experiences, we hope to contribute to the research discourse on peer leadership and point to fruitful spaces for future inquiry into the transformative potential of peer leadership.

First, peer leadership experiences should engage PLs in a significant investment of time and effort over an extended period. If our goal is to provide PLs with opportunities for deep and impactful learning, we cannot reduce peer leadership to a drop-in or fly-by experience. As we have highlighted, one practical application of this recommendation is to provide well-designed training that extends across the PL experience and that contributes to becoming. Additionally, campuses can structure PL roles in ways that allow students with interest and need to work up to 15 or 20 hours each week. Of course, simply punching a time clock does not guarantee learning. However, when institutions intentionally design the PL experience in ways that require PLs to make a significant investment of time and energy in meaningful activities, peer leadership can become a powerful way of addressing the working student dilemma (Burnside et al., 2019) by providing employment that provides both financial and academic benefit. While caution should be taken to avoid PL roles that require so much time as to negatively impact academic performance, research suggests that students can work up to approximately 15 hours each week without a decrease in academic performance (Burnside et al., 2019; Pike et al., 2008; Wenz & Yu, 2010).

Second, as with any other HIP, peer leadership should be an experience that offers PLs the chance to be part of a relationship-rich community (Felten & Lambert, 2020). This community should provide PLs with opportunities to develop both social and academic relationships by offering frequent interactions with the students they serve, their co-PLs, and supervising faculty or staff members. This community-based model of peer leadership helps PLs shift from the typical me-focused college experience to a we-focused orientation that enhances their sense of social and academic belonging, provides access to faculty and staff mentors, and fosters a feeling of shared purpose, as PLs see themselves participating in and contributing to the broader institutional mission (Young & Bunting, 2024). One way of fostering this sense of community is to organize PLs into standing cohorts that meet for training, gather informally to reflect on and grapple with challenges, and provide one another with feedback on one another's work. Similarly, structures should be in place that ensure that PLs meet regularly with a supervising staff or faculty member for feedback, reflection, and personalized support.

Third, we recommend that campuses consider pairing the PL experience with an accompanying credit-bearing course taught by a member of the faculty or staff who also serves in an administrative role for the program. Such a course can provide PLs with opportunities to study relevant student development theory; practice essential peer leadership skills; learn collaboratively with other PLs (e.g., through case studies, role play exercises, or simulations); and reflect on, articulate, and integrate the learning they are experiencing in the classroom and in their practice. In their discussion of the impact of compensation on PL outcomes, Young and Keup (2018) argued that the structure of an academic course—expectations of regular class attendance, frequent written assignments, opportunities for feedback on work, etc.—create an environment aligned with the characteristics of HIPs. Indeed, a course-based PL model organically incorporates accountability, feedback, reflection, interaction with faculty and peers, and public demonstration of learning in ways that are not as likely to occur in PL experiences without an accompanying course.

Fourth, we strongly urge institutional leaders to prioritize efforts to make meaningful PL experiences available to all students on their campus and to work to provide these opportunities as early as possible. As is apparent from the 2023 ISPL-US data, as well as past research (e.g., Bunting et al., 2012; Bunting & Williams, 2017; Harmon, 2006; Shook & Keup, 2012; Young et al., 2023), students who serve in well-designed PL roles stand to experience tremendous learning and growth. Consequently, institutional leaders have a moral and ethical obligation to ensure that these experiences are widely available. For example, an institution could create a campaign that broadly promotes the underlying message that "Peer leadership is for everyone," then target historically underrepresented student populations and engage academic advisors in helping students create a concise list of PL experiences they feel would be best to pursue. Similarly, campus units such as international student services, the office of inclusion and belonging, or a first-generation student organization, could collaborate with PL program administrators to nominate potential PLs.

Additionally, campuses need to find ways to offer sufficient compensation for PLs so that students with financial need do not face a choice between either earning enough money to survive, or becoming a PL. This is particularly important for students serving in FYE PL roles, given that they are more likely to report being eligible to receive Pell Grant funding. By reconceptualizing peer leadership as a student employment role, campuses are in a better position to both justify financial compensation for PLs and draw upon the research exploring student employment as a HIP. (See Burnside et al., 2019, for an excellent resource on designing high-impact student employment experiences.)

Finally, peer leadership is often reserved for students who are nearing the end of their college experience. Certainly, there are roles that require a degree of training and expertise that can only come with experience (e.g., being a teaching assistant for an upper-division course). However, students should not need to wait until their junior or senior year of college to have the types of high-impact PL experiences we have described in this chapter. In fact, given the impact that peer leadership seems to have on belonging and institutional connection, it would make sense for campuses to search for ways to provide these opportunities as early in their experience as possible, particularly for the most vulnerable students.

Conclusion and Directions for Future Research

In sum, we argue that (a) peer leadership should rightly be considered a HIP and (b) that there are particular elements of the PL experience—namely training, supervision, compensation, and reflection structures—that can significantly enhance the experience of the students who assume these roles.

Yet, there still remain a number of unanswered questions relative to the experience of FYE PLs. First, do PL outcomes vary depending on when a PL begins their experience? For example, do second-year students serving as PLs report similar outcomes as do senior students in PL roles? Second, how does the duration of PL experiences impact outcomes? Is a single semester in a PL role sufficient for them to experience growth? Or does the experience need to be longer? Finally, does the law of diminishing returns apply when it comes to PL growth and learning? In other words, would a PL be best served to remain in a single role across the duration of their experience or are they best served by seeking out a variety of PL experiences? We recommend that future research explore these and related questions.

While U.S. institutions have, historically, seen peer leadership programs as critical in supporting first-year and transfer students in becoming integrated into their new university communities, these programs offer the same benefit to those who serve as PLs. In fact, we argue that one of the most powerful ways that institutions might support students in transition is by finding ways for them to assume PL roles as early in their experience as possible. Indeed, becoming a PL seems to hold power in helping students feel as though they have become a true member of their campus community.

References

Bunting, B., Dye, B., Pinnegar, S., & Robinson, K. (2012). Understanding the dynamics of peer mentor learning: A narrative study. *Journal of the First-Year Experience & Students in Transition, 24*(1), 61-78.

Bunting, B., & Williams, D. (2017). Stories of transformation: Using personal narrative to explore transformative experience among undergraduate peer mentors. *Mentoring & Tutoring: Partnership in Learning, 25*(2), 166-184. https://psycnet.apa.org/doi/10.1080/13611267.2017.1327691

Burnside, O., Wesley, A., Wesaw, A., & Parnell, A. (2019). *Employing student success: A comprehensive examination of on-campus student employment.* NASPA-Student Affairs Administrators in Higher Education. https://www.naspa.org/report/employing-student-success-a-comprehensive-examination-of-on-campus-student-employment

Felten, P., & Lambert, L. M. (2020). *Relationship-rich education: How human connections drive success in college.* John Hopkins University Press.

Gopalan, M., & Brady, S. T. (2020). College students' sense of belonging: A national perspective. *Educational Researcher, 49*(2), 134-137. https://psycnet.apa.org/doi/10.3102/0013189X19897622

Greenfield, G. M., Keup, J. R., & Gardner, J. N. (2013). *Developing and sustaining successful first-year programs: A guide for practitioners.* John Wiley & Sons.

Harmon, B. (2006). A qualitative study of the learning processes and outcomes associated with students who serve as peer mentors. *Journal of the First-Year Experience & Students in Transition, 18*(2), 53-82.

Keup, J. R. (2020). Peer leadership, higher education. In P. N. Teixeira & J. C. Shin (Eds.), *The international encyclopedia of higher education systems and institutions* (pp. 2202-2210) https://doi.org/10.1007/978-94-017-8905-9_548

Kuh, G. D., & O'Donnell, K. (2013). Ensuring quality and taking high-impact practices to scale. *Peer Review, 15*(2), 32-33. https://link.gale.com/apps/doc/A339018909/AONE?u=byuprovo&sid=googleScholar&xid=39de3a32

Nunn, L. M. (2021). *College belonging: How first-year and first-generation students navigate campus life.* Rutgers University Press.

Pike, G. R., Kuh, G. D., & Massa-McKinley, R. C. (2008). First-year students' employment, engagement, and academic achievement: Untangling the relationship between work and grades. *NASPA Journal, 45*(4), 560-582. https://doi.org/10.2202/1949-6605.2011

Sanders, M. L. (2018). *Becoming a learner: Realizing the opportunity of education* (2nd ed). Hayden-McNeil. Schreiner, L. A., Louis, M. C., & Nelson, D. D. (Eds.). (2020). Thriving in transitions: A research-based approach to college student success. University of South Carolina, National Resource Center for The First-Year Experience and Students in Transition.

Shook, J. L., & Keup, J. R. (2012). The benefits of peer leader programs: An overview from the literature. *New Directions for Higher Education, 2012*(157), 5-16. https://doi.org/10.1002/he.20002

Strayhorn, T. L. (2019). *College students' sense of belonging: A key to educational success for all students* (2nd ed.). Routledge.

van der Meer, J., Skalicky, J., Speed, H., & Young, D. G. (2022). Focusing on the development of the whole student: An international comparative study of the perceived benefits of peer leadership in higher education. *Open Journal of Social Sciences, 10*(3), 14–35. https://doi.org/10.4236/jss.2022.103002

Wenz, M., & Yu, W. C. (2010). Term-time employment and the academic performance of undergraduates. *Journal of Education Finance,* 358-373.

Young, D. G., & Bunting, B. D. (2024). *Rethinking student transitions: How community, participation, and becoming can help higher education deliver on its promise.* University of South Carolina, National Resource Center for The First-Year Experience and Students in Transition.

Young, D. G., & Keup, J. R. (2018). To pay or not to pay: The influence of compensation as an external reward on learning outcomes of peer leaders. *Journal of College Student Development, 59*(2), 159-176. https://doi.org/10.1353/csd.2018.0015

Young, D. G., Zeng, W., Skalicky, J., & van der Meer, J. (2023). The quality and quantity of participation in peer leader experiences and student outcomes: A cross-national validation of constructs and predictive model. *Research in Higher Education,* 1-21. https://doi.org/10.1007/s11162-023-09765-4

Chapter 6

Peer Advising and Peer Advisors

Wendy G. Troxel
NACADA: The Global Community for Academic Advising

There is no lack of informal advising that goes on between students in colleges and universities. Students who have been at the institution for a year or two (or more) share insights, warnings, and opinions about the full range of experiences on campus and may even go as far as to provide technical and curricular information about life as a student. But while first-hand knowledge can be valuable, references to specific academic policies, procedures, and resources require intentional training and oversight. This section of the International Survey of Peer Leaders-US (ISPL-US) report addresses the academically focused role of Peer Advising and Peer Advisors. Situated within the context of academic advising in higher education more broadly, the practice of students serving students highlights key elements known to be high-impact, including

- Feedback on performance,
- Reflection and integration of learning,
- Written communication,
- Meaningful interactions with faculty & peers,
- Meaningful experiences with people and circumstances that differ from those with which students are familiar, and
- Investment of time (Kuh & O'Donnell, 2013).

This chapter addresses the emergence of peer leadership in academic advising and presents key findings from the ISPL-US, as well as observations and descriptions of an ongoing peer advising program in one institution in the United States. Finally, I present recommendations and implications for future structures and strategies that promote learning for students who serve as peer leaders (PLs).

The Emergence of Peer Leaders in Academic Advising

The role of academic advising gained traction in the United States in the early 1970s, when Crookston (1972) distinguished between developmental and prescriptive strategies for helping students navigate their college experience. His focus on active learning highlighted this student-centered practice in a deeper way than the service-orientated, clerical functions of scheduling and enrollment. Over the last 50 years, the literature related to academic advising has continued to grow, describing a wide range of approaches to the work, supported by learning and development theory and documentable instructional strategies toward intended outcomes of student learning across every discipline (Drake et al., 2013; Hagen, 2018; Johnson et al., 2023).

As institutions compete for students, and society continues to hold colleges and universities accountable for increased rates of persistence, retention, and completion, support for students is more important than ever. Professional associations such as NACADA: The Global Community for Academic Advising, provide focused guidance for the work of full-time academic advisors (often referred to as primary-role advisors) and faculty members who provide advising to students. NACADA's Core Values (2017) describe "the many cultural and educational contexts in which academic advising is practiced globally" (para. 1). An increasing number of standards of practice further encourage colleges and universities to situate academic advising within the teaching and learning mission of the institution, including the CAS Standards (2022) and the Conditions of Excellence in Academic Advising (NACADA, 2023). Of particular interest to the focused practice of academic advising, NACADA's Core Competencies (2022) delineate key components in three major areas: (a) informational—addressing the locally contextual knowledge that academic advisors must master, (b) relational—highlighting the interpersonal nature of advising interactions, and (c) conceptual—focusing on the concepts and theories required for the role.

Some institutions have turned to peer advising because of its multi-layered benefits related to efficiency (informational), effectiveness (relational), and impact (conceptual). Peer advising programs are efficient simply because they provide more help to students across the institution seeking academic information (Zabel & Rothberger, 2012). Peer advising programs are effective because they place trusted, trained student staff members close to students, providing authentic peer-to-peer relationships (Latino & Unite, 2012). Peer advising programs are impactful because the peer advisors (students) gain experience and skills that lead to deeper conceptual growth in areas related to leadership skills, teaching techniques, learning outcomes, and critical thinking (Kau & Tagorda, 2016). They should also involve elements of contextual training and content knowledge, and professional development addressing continuous personal and career-oriented improvement (Sancar et al., 2021).

Findings from the ISPL-US for Peer Advisors

The ISPL-US report provided data for those undergraduate students who serve or have served in the role of peer advisor at their institution. I have categorized findings by demographic information, specific peer advising experiences and structures, and perceptions of skills gained (which I explore further through the framework of informational, relational, and conceptual competencies).

Demographic Information

Out of the 1,531 students who responded to the ISPL study, 292 indicated that they were serving ($n = 278$) or had served ($n = 14$) as a peer advisor. As discussed previously, they were enrolled in a wide variety of academic majors, with most coming from the "social sciences" ($n = 66, 22.6\%$), "business, management, marketing, and support services" ($n = 46, 15.8\%$), and "health professional and related programs" ($n = 44, 15.1\%$). Peer advisor respondents indicated over two dozen additional areas of study, with two students reporting that they were currently "undeclared."

Reported Cumulative GPA

Not surprisingly, most of the peer advisors reported cumulative GPAs of over 3.00 ($n = 264, 93.6\%$). This is likely due to the academic requirements of the application process to become a peer advisor. Most reported that they live off campus ($n = 183, 62.9\%$), which is slightly higher than the overall sample report of 54.0%. This is likely due to the nature of the peer advising position which often requires that students have completed at least one full year at the institution. The peer advisors who responded to the ISPL study were mostly in their third or fourth year in higher education ($n = 173, 59.3\%$), with 77 (26.4%) students in their second year.

Personal Identities

Regarding personal identity, most peer advisors were not first-generation students, with 71.8% indicating that at least one parent or guardian earned a college degree. Their eligibility for financial aid under the Pell Grant program mirrored the overall responses for the study (see Table 6.1).

Table 6.1

Respondents Eligible for Financial Aid Under the Pell Grant program (n = 292)

Pell eligibilty	PL type Academic - Peer advisor		All respondents	
	Freq.	%	Freq.	%
Yes	104	35.6	476	31.2
No	130	44.5	677	44.3
I don't know	58	19.9	375	24.5

Age and Residency Status

The highest percentage of peer advisors are between the ages of 21 and 25 (n = 171, 58.6%) with the next highest percentage of peer advisors between the ages of 18 and 20 (n = 112, 38.4%). Most reported enrollment at their institution as an in-state student (n = 206, 70.5%), which is slightly higher than the results overall (64.5%). This may relate to feelings of confidence and familiarity with the institution and its geographical location, which may lead students to seek opportunities to help other students navigate their cultural and physical environments.

Gender, Race, and Ethnicity

Most of the peer advisor respondents identified as women (n = 206, 70.5%), consistent with the overall results of this study (67.8%). Most respondents reported their race or ethnicity as White (n = 211, 72.3%). The second highest percentage of peer advisors reported their race or ethnicity as Hispanic, Chicano/a, or Latino/a (n = 55, 18.8%). The breakdown of race or ethnicity is important to consider within the context of opportunity and representation in higher education (see Table 6.2). Just over 24% (24.3%) reported that they are a member of an historically oppressed racial or ethnic group.

The demographics of peer advisors who participated in the ISPL-US are quite consistent with national statistics on professional advisors. Zippia (2023) reported that "64.7% of all academic advisers [sic] are women, while 35.5% are men" (para. 2) and a combined 24.8% reported that they are Hispanic or Latino (14.2%), or Black or African American (10.6%). While there is evidence that the gender of the academic advisor does influence persistence for women students in STEM fields (Canaan & Mouganie, 2023; Gaule & Piacentini, 2018), and Students of Color benefit from advisors who serve them through advocacy (Lee, 2018) and equitable practices (Museus, 2021), there is little research on why most academic advisors are White women. Academic advising may attract more women in similar ways that other helping professions like education and nursing do, highlighting key factors that lead to gender imbalances in the workforce, including cultural conditioning, peer pressure, and personality traits related to nurturing and caring (Leach, 2016).

Do undergraduate students who seek roles in peer leadership, and particularly peer advising, naturally gravitate toward positions where they see professionals who look like they do, or have had positive experiences with academic advisors, or because they are naturally suited to the higher education environment? If so, does the traditional peer advisor context benefit White females by design, further exacerbating the dominant culture (regarding race and gender) of academic advising as a profession? The field needs more research in this area, but institutions offering peer advising opportunities should consider the implicit and explicit messages related to the recruitment and support of a pool of students with a variety of backgrounds to become a part of the program.

Table 6.2
Academic Peer Advisor Demographics by Race or Ethnicity (n = 318)

Race or Ethnicity	PL type Academic - Peer advisor		All respondents	
	Freq.	%	Freq.	%
American Indian or Alaska Native	3	1.0	15	1.0
Asian or Asian American	21	7.2	134	8.8
Black or African American	17	5.8	107	7.0
Hispanic, Chicano/a, or Latino/a	55	18.8	229	15.0
Native Hawaiian or other Pacific Islander	1	0.3	13	0.9
White	211	72.3	1127	74.0
Other:	6	2.1	27	1.8
Preferred not to respond	4	1.4	20	1.3

Note. Respondents selected all that applied.

Peer Advising Experiences and Structures

Most of the peer advisors in this data set were relatively new to the role, indicating they had completed one semester/term (n = 97, 33.4%) or two semesters/terms (n = 69, 23.8%). Peer advisors in this study also reported a wide range of peer leadership experiences as well, with the highest involvement in the first-year experience (n = 119, 40.8%), as well as experience in student clubs and organizations (n = 84, 28.8%) and orientation (n = 65, 22.3%). Peer advisors are heavily involved in leadership positions overall, though, having held multiple positions throughout their college career (see Table 6.3).

Additionally, almost half reported that they have served as a senior PL or in another supervisory role (n = 114, 41.8%). These data may suggest that, compared to the broader survey population, peer advisors come into their role with slightly more experience in other PL roles. This may be due to position requirements related to class rank (for example, peer advisors need to have completed at least one year of college). Students drawn to these types of roles may first seek out other PL opportunities in the first year to gain experience which may then lead to more advanced PL roles, like academic advising.

Compensation

Most peer advisors reported that they received "financial compensation such as an hourly wage or stipend" (n = 256, 90.5%). Future studies should separate forms of compensation, particularly "hourly wage" and "stipend" to explore implications related to commitment, engagement, and professionalism. Anecdotally, for example, one director of a peer advising program has observed higher levels of no shows, lower levels of engagement, and higher levels of turnover in peer advisors since changing from a stipend (dispensed each term, with conditions and expectations attached) to an hourly rate (Eve Millet, personal correspondence, September 29, 2023).

Table 6.3
Total Peer Leader Positions Held During Their University Experience (n = 288)

Number of PL positions	PL type Academic - Peer advisor		All respondents	
	Freq.	%	Freq.	%
1	77	26.7	507	37.4
2	71	24.7	318	23.5
3	49	17.0	225	16.6
4	27	9.4	107	7.9
5	18	6.3	84	6.2
6	18	6.3	53	3.9
7	12	4.2	27	2.0
8	6	2.1	12	0.9
9	3	1.0	6	0.4
10 or more	7	2.4	16	1.2

Training and Professional Development

The peer advisors reported similar patterns of engagement with both initial and ongoing training and professional development as did the broader sample of participants. Initial training varied from a half day or less through three or more weeks. Results are unclear regarding the structure of the individual peer advising programs and the amount and frequency of initial training and ongoing professional development. Interestingly, a small number of peer advisors reported "no additional ongoing formal training after the initial training" ($n = 42$, 15.1%) but that may be related to initial training that lasted multiple weeks. Those who reported that they did participate in additional formal training indicated a range of activities (see Table 6.4), most of which involved interactions with supervisors and colleagues.

Time On Task and Modalities

These peer advisors reported working a higher number of hours per week than the overall group of respondents in the ISPL-US, with more indicating that they work between 11 and 20 hours ($n = 136$, 47.2% vs. 41.0%, respectively). While some advising sessions occur online, most happened in person. Further study may include inquiries related to these elements, including the extent to which peer advising is effective in person or online, based on the nature of the student-to-student interactions. Issues of confidentiality, accountability, and environment also warrant deeper exploration.

Ongoing Feedback on Performance

The majority of peer advisors report that they do receive regular opportunities to receive feedback on their performance in the role ($n = 219$, 77.1%). This aligns with Kuh & O'Donnell's (2013) key elements of high impact practices (HIPs). Conversely, 49 ($n = 49$) reported that they do not receive feedback on their performance, and 16 ($n = 16$) respondents reported that they "don't know" if they receive feedback (effectively a "no" response). Most meetings related to their performance occur with a supervising faculty or staff member ($n = 175$, 80.6%).

Reflections are an important aspect of learning and development, and most report that they engage in those types of activities ($n = 219$; 80.6%). Programs that do not offer an opportunity to reflect on, articulate, or integrate learning experiences in this type of role are missing a critical element of effective leadership.

Table 6.4

Additional Ongoing Formal Training Received (n = 231)

	PL type Academic - Peer advisor		All respondents	
Training	**Freq.**	**%**	**Freq.**	**%**
Regular meetings specifically dedicated to train-ing, such as workshops	187	81.0%	727	76.9%
Training during staff meetings	130	56.3%	485	51.3%
Training during meetings with supervisor	107	46.3%	389	41.2%
Periodic refresher sessions (e.g., prior to or during semester)	99	42.9%	374	39.6%
Online or asynchronous self-paced training	72	31.2%	299	31.6%
Training during a retreat	64	27.7%	225	23.8%
Other (please specify):	3	1.3%	22	2.3%

Note. Respondents selected all that applied.

Motivation to Become a Peer Advisor

Undergraduate students who seek out positions of leadership do so for several reasons. Not surprisingly, "to help or benefit other students" ranked highest in the list of reasons these respondents chose to serve as peer advisors ($n = 262$, 91.9%), followed by, "to share my knowledge/experience with others ($n = 238$, 83.5%), and "for personal/professional challenges and skill development" ($n = 226$, 79.3%). The opportunity to earn income as a peer advisor ranked fourth on the list ($n = 203$, 71.2%). These students appear to recognize the role of academic advising as one of support and mentoring. They also recognize that the role has the potential to help them develop skills and to challenge them both personally and professionally.

Perception of Skills Gained

Peer leadership roles intentionally promote a wide range of skills and abilities. The ISPL-US respondents in the peer advisor role reported significant gains in all areas. Overall, peer advisors reported the highest gains in "your knowledge of campus resources" (91.1% increased or greatly increased). This is not surprising, since the advising role itself focuses on assisting and advising students to access resources and more effectively use them toward higher levels of success. Additionally, peer advisors reported increased or greatly increased gains in leadership (84.6%), interpersonal communication (81.7%), interaction with people different than themselves (81.3%), and meaningful interaction with peers (81.0%).

When compared to the total set of respondents in peer leadership roles, peer advisors reported skills gained at a higher level in every category except one: "meaningful interaction with staff members" (-1.3 percentage point difference). This may be due to the significantly higher reported gains in "meaningful interactions with faculty members" (7.9 percentage points higher) and "meaningful interactions with peers" (3.8 percentage points higher). The extent to which peer advisors report higher levels of skill development and growth than other PL positions is worthy of further study. This may be due to factors such as timing (most peer advisors are sophomores and beyond), differences in training and supervision (given the complexity of the role related to institutional policies and procedures), and compensation (rates may be higher than other PL positions). Further exploration of specific skills related to peer advising would be of benefit to the field.

While not structured this way in the survey, I will also explore the results of the ISPL-US through the lens of the NACADA (2022) Core Competencies of informational, relational, and conceptual, as described earlier.

Informational Component

The informational component "refers to the knowledge that advisors must gain to guide the students at their institution" (Folsom et al., 2015, p. 6). It includes information related to a wide range of institutional policies, programs, and services. Advisors learn these specific elements through training and professional development, so the skills necessary to be successful at the role include things such as time management, organizational skills, written skills, and others (see Table 6.5). While the peer advisors report higher levels of gain in each area as compared to the PL respondents overall, it is interesting to note that the role generally does not include written communication. Again, it is not surprising that "knowledge of campus resources" rates highest in the informational area of competencies.

Table 6.5

Degree to Which the Following Informational Skills Changed as a Direct Result of Peer Leadership Experiences (n = 279)

	Increased or greatly increased			
	PL type Academic - Peer advisor		All responses	Difference
Informational Skill	**Freq.**	**%**	**%**	**%**
Your knowledge of campus resources	247	91.1	84.8	6.3
Time management	211	77.6	72.7	4.9
Organizational	206	74.9	70.2	4.7
Project management	194	70.3	66.5	3.8
Presentation	182	66.2	59.1	7.9
Written communication	161	58.5	52.5	6.0
Sharing ideas with others in writing	143	53.4	48.3	5.1

Relational Component

Done well, academic advising is relational in nature. It "involves the communicative skills and interpersonal approaches advisors must build, including those critical to establishing advising relationships with students" (Folsom et al., 2015, p. 6). The elements in Table 6.6 reveal important skills addressed in peer leadership, with particular focus on the peer advising role. While "interpersonal communication" rates highest in this area, some students who are peer advisors are likely already confident in their skills to relate to others. Of note, however, is the element "your interaction with people with backgrounds different than your own," with peer advisors rating this element at a higher level than did the total pool of respondents (a difference of 9.1 percentage points). This element again highlights peer advising as a high impact practice (Kuh & O'Donnell, 2013).

Table 6.6

Degree to Which the Following Relational Skills Changed as a Direct Result of Peer Leadership Experiences (n = 279)

| | Increased or greatly increased | | | |
| | PL type Academic - Peer advisor | | All responses | Difference |
Relational Skill	Freq.	%	%	%
Interpersonal communication	223	81.7	80.7	1.0
Your interaction with people with backgrounds different than your own	221	81.3	72.2	9.1
Your meaningful interaction with peers	218	81.0	77.2	3.8
Teamwork and collaboration	217	79.5	77.5	2.0
Building relationships with people with whom you work	212	79.1	77.1	2.0
Your feeling that you belong and are welcome at your institution	189	68.9	66.3	2.6
Providing direction through interpersonal persuasion	179	65.3	61.0	4.3
Your meaningful interaction with faculty	177	63.9	56.0	7.9

Conceptual Component

The conceptual component addresses "the ideas and theories that advisors must understand to effectively practice the art" (Folsom et al., 2015, p. 6). of academic advising. Students who train to become peer advisors must develop professional skills, abilities, and dispositions that lead to deeper understanding of themselves, of others, and of the context and environments of higher education. Reflection on how they have grown has implications for personal and professional maturity, as well as increased ability to translate skills to other current and future situations.

Table 6.7 reveals that peer advisors reported increased or greatly increased skill gains at higher levels than the aggregated totals in key areas, including "critical thinking" (9.4 percentage point difference) and "your interaction with people with backgrounds different than your own" (9.1 percentage points higher).

Additionally, most peer advisors reported no change or slightly increased change to their GPA (65%), number of credit hours (64.9%), time to expected graduation (82.0%), and overall academic performance (63.6%). These responses were consistent with the overall aggregated results for the study. Also consistent with the overall responses, peer advisors highly recommend peer leadership to others (see Table 6.8). Finally, 89.3% (*n* = 242) of peer advisors were satisfied or very satisfied with their peer leadership experiences, slightly higher than the overall results of the study (86.1%).

Table 6.7

Degree to Which the Following Conceptual Skills Changed as a Direct Result of Peer Leadership Experiences (n = 279)

| | Increased or greatly increased | | | |
| | PL type Academic - Peer advisor | | All responses | Difference |
Conceptual Skill	**Freq.**	**%**	**%**	**%**
Your feeling that you are contributing to your campus community	222	80.1	76.6	3.5
Leadership	231	84.6	83.1	1.5
Adaptability	219	79.0	77.3	1.7
Your knowledge about people with backgrounds different than your own	213	77.5	70.1	6.4
Your understanding of people with backgrounds different than your own	211	77.3	69.6	7.7
Critical thinking	216	73.8	64.4	9.4
Your meaningful interaction with staff members	202	73.5	74.8	-1.3
Problem solving	202	72.9	68.2	4.7
Bringing together information learned from different places	194	72.4	66.4	6.0
Applying knowledge to a real-world setting through hands-on experiences	190	71.1	68.8	2.9
Decision-making	189	68.7	67.3	1.4
Analyzing a problem from new perspectives	178	65.9	64.8	1.1
Creating innovative approaches to complete a task	178	65.9	59.8	6.1
Engaging in ethical decision-making	171	63.8	60.0	3.8
Creativity	172	61.6	58.4	3.2
Your desire to stay at your institution and graduate	165	60.4	58.6	1.8
Your desire to engage in continuous learning following graduation	165	60.4	57.0	3.4

Table 6.8

Responses Describing if Participants Would Recommend Being a PL to Other Students (n = 271)

| | PL type Academic - peer advisor | | Total | |
Recommendation	**Freq.**	**%**	**Freq.**	**%**
Yes, absolutely	202	74.5	940	73.8
Yes, for most of the peer leadership positions I have held	47	17.3	221	17.4
Yes, for some of the peer leadership positions I have held (but not most)	15	5.5	66	5.2
No or I don't know (responses combined)	7	2.6	46	3.6

Key Considerations

While this study did not assess the effectiveness of the peer advising programs themselves, the results provide evidence of the quality of peer advisors' experience. Responses reveal that peer advising involves several of the characteristics of HIPs (Kuh & O'Donnell, 2013), including:

- Feedback on performance: Over 77% (77.1%) said they do receive regular opportunities to receive feedback on their performance as peer advisors.

- Reflection and integration of learning: Over 78% (78.8%) of the respondents reported that they were "provided with periodic structured opportunities to reflect on, articulate, or integrate the learning [they] were experiencing as a PL" in the role of academic advising.

- Written communication: Just over half (58.5%) of the peer advisors reported that their skills "increased or greatly increased" around written communication.

- Meaningful interactions with faculty and peers: PLs reported structured interactions with faculty members and staff at a high rate (80.6%), and the role itself focuses primarily on peer interactions. The vast majority (91.9%) reported that they chose to take on the role in order "to help or benefit other students."

- Meaningful experiences with people and circumstances that differ from their own: Peer advisors reported that their skills increased or greatly increased relative to the item, "Your interaction with people with backgrounds different than your own" (81.3%).

- Investment of time: Most peer advisors (83.2%) reported working between 6 and 20 hours per week in the role (6-10 = 26.0%; 11-15 = 21.5%; 16-20 = 25.7%). (Note: respondents were instructed to select all that apply and to consider all of the PL roles they had held during college; consequently, percentages do not add up to 100%.)

The results of the ISPL-US also suggest that peer advising is a pathway to contextual belonging, deep engagement, and personal and professional goal setting. Providing leadership opportunities for students with minoritized races and ethnicities not only encourages deeper connections with fellow students but encourages the potential for a more diverse workforce in the helping professions of higher education, such as academic advising.

Conclusions and Implications

Readers should consider a number of key questions related to peer advising. First is the question, "How can institutional leaders continue to refine and improve the design of peer advising experiences to align with what is known about high-impact practices (HIPs)?" Indeed, there were troubling results in the ISPL-US data regarding peer advising. Nearly one in five respondents reported little interaction with faculty and staff (n = 42, 19.4%), and little opportunity to reflect on their experiences (n = 60, 21.2%). Of note were responses that suggested that both initial training and ongoing follow-up occurred on a limited basis. Future studies should also seek to delineate between activities meant to train the peer advisors on policies, procedures, and practices and activities focused on their ongoing professional development (Sancar et al., 2021). This role has direct connections to the profession of academic advising in higher education, as well as future careers that will require similar engagement with problem-solving, interpersonal communication, and leadership.

The second question higher education professionals should ask is, "Which students are currently being excluded from these experiences?" Academic leaders should critically determine the extent to which institutions are summarily excluding students from minoritized identities and backgrounds from these types of experiences, or if these students themselves resist these experiences due to lack of engagement with staff and faculty who relate to them. Anecdotally, some institutions still use peer advisors as cheap labor, neglecting the obligation to provide deep learning experiences to the peer advisors themselves. There is clear similarity to experiential or applied learning programs, such as internships and practica (DuVall et al., 2018). Students involved in the peer advising program should leave the institution with a focused portfolio of demonstrated experiences and skills gained. Findings from the ISPL-US offer evidence that key elements of HIPs as noted above provide a learning environment that leads to meaningful personal and professional growth.

Additionally, institutions should carefully consider who applies to their peer advising programs. They should be on the lookout for students who may be overly involved. There may be a tendency to select those who have considerable experience in peer leadership roles (e.g., White females), and those who appear to have little challenge in school. Institutions must intentionally recruit peer advisors with a wide range of identities and backgrounds. Doing so may also nurture deeper and more widespread interactions between students and their advisors, potentially raising interest in the role on campus. Staff, faculty, and students who have been minoritized or who have struggled academically but have experienced success often provide effective, long-lasting support to others (Castellanos & Jones, 2023).

I offer the following recommendations for institutions seeking to create and sustain strong peer advising programs:

- Identify the essential components of the peer advising experience for each institution, including practical elements related to type and form of compensation, modalities for delivery of services, and intended outcomes for learning and development,

- Acknowledge and address the varied strategies necessary to respond to a diverse student population (Troxel & Kyei-Blankson, 2018),

- Identify the challenges and opportunities associated with peer advising at their institution. Explore and evaluate the extent to which students can serve in peer leadership roles that brings meaning and impact for the peer advisors, students who benefit from their expertise, and the staff and faculty who collaborate with them as mentors and colleagues. Furthest from the list of benefits should be the goal of cheap labor to help overburdened staff and faculty,

- Engage in dialogue with colleagues about the implications of the survey findings related to the mission, vision, and goals of the academic advising program at the institution. This can happen through focused conversations with key institutional partners, particularly when these conversations occur alongside common readings and strategic planning processes,

- Consider how this experience leads to growth and engagement in goal setting and career exploration for peer advisors and other students in leadership positions. Systematic and systemic assessment practices should include evidence of learning as a direct result of peer advising activities, and

- Intentionally structure contextual experiences for students who seek leadership positions, including experiences that address issues of power, privacy, roles, and scope. Interrogate institutional policies and procedures to highlight a vocal, transparent commitment to breaking the patterns of traditional dominant culture. Examine both implicit and explicit messages surrounding the recruitment and training for the peer advising program. Actively seek students from a range of backgrounds and identities, and highlight key elements, contexts, and strategies related to socially just academic advising for all students.

Peer advisors have significant potential to positively support every student, in every academic program at an institution. Institutions that fully embrace the strengths, abilities, and perspectives of their community members (students, staff, and faculty) create powerful environments for meaningful, continuous, and collaborative learning.

References

Canaan, S., & Mouganie, P. (2023). The impact of advisor gender on female students' STEM enrollment and persistence. *Journal of Human Resources, 58*(2), 593-632. https://doi.org/10.3368/jhr.58.4.0320-10796R2

Castellanos, J., & Jones, L. (Eds.). (2023). *The majority in the minority: Expanding the representation of Latina/o faculty, administrators and students in higher education.* Taylor & Francis.

Council for the Advancement of Standards in Higher Education. (2023). Academic advising functional area. https://www.cas.edu/standards.html

Crookston, B. B. (1972). A developmental view of academic advising as teaching. *Journal of College Student Personnel, 13*, 12-17.

Drake, J. K., Jordan, P., & Miller, M. A. (2013). *Academic advising approaches: Strategies that teach students to make the most of college* (1st ed.). Jossey-Bass.

DuVall, K. D. R., Rininger, A., & Sliman, A. T. (2018, December). Peer advising: Building a professional undergraduate advising practicum. *Academic Advising Today, 41*(4). https://nacada.ksu.edu/Resources/Academic-Advising-Today/View-Articles/Peer-Advising-Building-a-Professional-Undergraduate-Advising-Practicum.aspx

Folsom, P., Yoder, F., & Joslin, J. (2015). *New advisor guidebook: Mastering the art of academic advising* (2nd ed.). Wiley.w

Gaule, P., & Piacentini, M. (2018). An advisor like me? Advisor gender and post-graduate careers in science. *Research Policy, 47*(4), 805-813. https://doi.org/10.1016/j.respol.2018.02.011

Hagen, P. L. (2018). *The power of story: Narrative theory in academic advising.* NACADA: The Global Community for Academic Advising.

Johnson, R. M., Strayhorn, T. L., & Travers, C. S. (2023). Examining the academic advising experiences of Black males at an urban university: An exploratory case study. *Urban Education, 58*(5), 774-800. https://doi.org/10.1177/0042085919894048

Kau, C., & Tagorda, M. (2016, March). Peer to professional: Navigating the transition. *Academic Advising Today, 39*(1). https://nacada.ksu.edu/Resources/Academic-Advising-Today/View-Articles/Peer-to-Professional-Navigating-the-Transition.aspx

Kuh, G. D., O'Donnell, K., & Reed, S. (2013). *Ensuring quality and taking high impact practices to scale.* Association of American Colleges & Universities. https://www.aacu.org/publication/ensuring-quality-and-taking-high-impact-practices-to-scale

Latino, J. A., & Unite, C. M. (2012). Providing academic support through peer education. *New Directions for Higher Education, 2012*(157), 31-43.

Leach, D. (2016, Nov 30). Why is nursing a predominantly female occupation? *Challenge Magazine.* https://www.challengemagazine.com/other/finance-career/why-is-nursing-a-predominantly-female-occupation/

Lee, J. A. (2018). Affirmation, support, and advocacy. Critical Race Theory and academic advising. *NACADA Journal, 38*(1), 77-87. https://doi.org/10.12930/NACADA-17-028

Museus, S. D. (2021). Revising the role of academic advising in equitably serving diverse college students. *NACADA Journal, 41*(1), 26-32. https://doi.org/10.12930/NACADA-21-06

NACADA: The Global Community for Academic Advising (2006). NACADA concept of academic advising. https://nacada.ksu.edu/Resources/Pillars/Concept.aspx

NACADA: The Global Community for Academic Advising (2017). NACADA Core values of academic advising. https://nacada.ksu.edu/Resources/Pillars/CoreValues.aspx

NACADA: The Global Community for Academic Advising (2022). NACADA academic advising core competencies model. https://nacada.ksu.edu/Resources/Pillars/CoreCompetencies.aspx

NACADA: The Global Community for Academic Advising (2023). The conditions of excellence in academic advising. https://nacada.ksu.edu/Programs/Excellence-in-Academic-Advising.aspx

Sancar, R., Atal, D., & Deryakulu, D. (2021, March). A new framework for teachers' professional development. *Teaching and Teacher Education, 101*, 103305. https://doi.org/10.1016/j.tate.2021.103305

Troxel, W. G., & Kyei-Blankson, L. (2018). *The "typical" advising session: An exploration of consistency.* NACADA: The Global Community for Academic Advising.

Zabel, L., & Rothberger, S. (2012). Peer advising: Bridging the gap between professional advisor and students. *Academic Advising Today, 35*(2). https://www.nacada.ksu.edu/Resources/Academic-Advising-Today/View-Articles/Peer-Advising-Bridging-the-Gap-Between-Professional-Advisor-and-Student.aspx

Zippia. (2023). Academic adviser demographics and statistics in the US. *Zippia Career Platform.* https://www.zippia.com/academic-adviser-jobs/demographics/

Chapter 7

The Impact of Peer Leadership in Supplemental Instruction

Kate Verheyn
University of West Georgia

Jessica Pearson
International Center for Supplemental Instruction

As we sifted through the student responses to the 2023 International Survey of Peer Leaders administered in the United States (ISPL-US), we quickly recognized evidence that Supplemental Instruction (SI) Leaders are gaining important skills that the International Center for Supplemental Instruction (ICSI) encourages SI programs to impart to their leaders. We begin this chapter by reviewing the history and structure of the SI program, which we believe is fundamental to understanding the key findings from the ISPL-US data relative to SI Leaders. We have highlighted three key themes from the data: the essential nature of the training and support SI Leaders receive; the communities with which SI Leaders engage; and the skills that SI Leaders gain in the course of their employment. At the end of this chapter, we provide our recommendations based on our combined experiences as former SI Leaders, SI supervisors, and continued work with ICSI.

History of Supplemental Instruction

In 1973, Dr. Deanna Martin created SI at the University of Missouri-Kansas City (UMKC). SI is a peer-led academic support program that enhances student performance and retention. This initiative emerged due to increased enrollment and varied academic readiness after the University of Kansas City joined the University of Missouri System in 1963. At this time UMKC was an "inner-city, commuter institution" that "typically turned over 40% of its students each semester" (Martin & Arendale, 1992, p.42). Consequently, Dr. Martin, then a UMKC School of Education graduate student, aimed to improve student preparedness for the workforce and post-graduate studies through the implementation of the SI program.

Recognized as an Exemplary Program by the U.S. Department of Education in 1983 and 1992, SI received funding and validation for wider implementation (Martin & Arendale, 1992). Certified SI Trainers spread the model in the 1990s, leading to its global expansion under names like Peer Assisted Study Sessions (PASS) and Peer Assisted Learning (PAL). UMKC launched the International Center for Supplemental Instruction (ICSI) in 1999 in response to SI's global expansion and popularity. Today, national Centers in various countries—including Sweden, South Africa, Australia, and Canada—further promote SI training, innovation, and best practices.

In 2018, Certified Trainers from the National Centers and the International Center developed a comprehensive definition for SI:

Supplemental Instruction (SI) is a non-remedial approach to learning that supports students toward academic success by integrating "what to learn" with "how to learn." SI consists of regularly scheduled,

"

voluntary, out-of-class group study sessions driven by students' needs. Sessions are facilitated by trained peer leaders who utilize collaborative activities to ensure peer-to-peer interaction in small groups. SI is implemented in high-risk courses in consultation with academic staff and is supported and evaluated by a trained supervisor. (The Curators of the University of Missouri, 2019, p. 8)

Program Structure

The SI program places a strong emphasis on SI Leader training and support and meaningful interactions with the campus community. The ICSI supports and develops SI Leaders through a set of standard program guidelines, which include pre-term and ongoing training sessions, observations, and continuous feedback. These peer leaders (PLs) engage in earnest relationships with faculty, programmatic staff members, and other students to put forth successful SI sessions.

The characteristics of high-impact practices (HIPs), identified by Kuh and O'Donnell (2013) and discussed in Chapter 2, align with the guidelines established by ICSI. The characteristics of HIPs also reinforce the importance of adhering closely to the SI program's suggested structure. We see particularly strong connections with the characteristics of high expectations; meaningful interactions with faculty and peers; frequent, timely and constructive feedback; and public demonstration of competence.

The ICSI recommends that SI programs provide SI Leaders with a robust pre-term training covering topics such as facilitation strategies, collaborative learning techniques, learning strategies, marketing strategies, session planning, and other program-related activities. This approach illustrates the high expectations that are present throughout the overall training structure of SI. Further, this pre-term training should provide an opportunity for new and returning SI Leaders to roleplay at least one mock SI session to prepare for scenarios they may encounter during the semester (Hoiland et al., 2020). Following the pre-term training, SI Leaders should engage in ongoing professional development. Topics of these ongoing sessions may include troubleshooting complex student situations, working across student differences, and personal development outside of SI. The International Center further recommends inviting campus partners to ongoing training sessions to better prepare SI Leaders to connect their attendees with the appropriate resources. No matter the topic, the International Center emphasizes the importance of having a clear agenda or goals for the training (The Curators of the University of Missouri, 2019).

Along with ongoing training sessions, SI Leaders should receive regular feedback on their sessions through observations and debriefs throughout the semester. The Curators of the University of Missouri (2019) recommend that supervisors or senior leaders observe the first three sessions for all SI Leaders, with weekly observations for new SI Leaders and biweekly observations for returning SI leaders for the remainder of the semester. Following an observation, the SI Leader meets with their observer in an official debrief session to discuss their opportunities for improvement. This iterative process of observation, feedback, and reflection is well-aligned with the characteristics of HIPs and significantly enhances SI Leader learning.

Following the pre-term training, SI Leaders begin to work closely with the faculty member(s) for their assigned course. This working relationship is crucial for the success of the SI sessions, as faculty are supportive partners in garnering student buy-in and identifying important session topics. Instructors are further able to support the SI program by promoting their SI Leader's review sessions, which may boost attendance (Hurley et al., 2006). While attendance at SI sessions is anonymous to the professor, the SI Leader can offer valuable insights to the faculty member about topics with which students appear to be struggling. SI Leaders' regular interactions with faculty are another example of how SI practice aligns with the characteristics of HIPs. Further, this expert-novice model embodies the key structural elements of *legitimate peripheral participation* (Lave & Wenger, 1991) and sets SI Leaders up for meaningful forms of personal growth and becoming (Young & Bunting, 2024) as described in Chapter 2 of this report.

Equally important, SI Leaders also work in close relation to programmatic staff members. These individuals are usually responsible for the hiring, training, and development of SI Leaders. They manage the overall operations of the SI program by ensuring that SI Leaders have a space in which to hold their sessions, scheduling ongoing training sessions for the student staff, serving as a bridge between faculty and the SI Leaders, and collecting and analyzing SI data (Hurley et al., 2006).

This type of high-quality supervision of SI Leaders is critical. Burmeister and Martin (1996) noted how active supervision holds SI Leaders accountable and prevents them from shifting from facilitating to tutoring or lecturing during their review sessions. Fostering a positive and collaborative learning environment is foundational to the SI model. Supervising staff members play a key role in effectively training SI Leaders on how to build such an environment and ensure SI Leaders have access to the resources they need to plan and facilitate their sessions. As described previously, staff supervisors also provide essential feedback on SI Leader performance through ongoing observations.

SI Leaders also engage in meaningful interactions with both the students who participate in their SI sessions, as well as senior SI Leaders. These senior leaders are veterans in the role and provide training and support to those newer in the role (again, in alignment with the core tenets of *legitimate peripheral participation;* Lave & Wenger, 1991). Senior leaders operate under various names depending on the institution, but they are typically known as Peer Mentors. The Curators of the University of Missouri (2019) provide the following qualifications for Peer Mentors:

> Applicants must have been successful SI Leaders for two semesters and must demonstrate knowledge of the SI program and adherence to the model. Applicants must also show exceptional SI planning and facilitation skills and excellent leadership skills (p. 73).

Institutions may deviate from these qualifications as they see fit, but the general responsibilities of senior leaders, regardless of their official title, include assisting in pre-term and ongoing training sessions, conducting observations of fellow SI Leaders, and providing feedback on session planning sheets.

Key Findings

In the following discussion of the results of the 2023 ISPL-US we highlight (a) the demographic profile of SI Leaders in the sample, (b) the nature of the training and support SI Leaders reported receiving, (c) the sense of community and belonging reported by SI Leaders, and (d) the overall impact of SI leadership upon SI Leaders as students and PLs. Additionally, we discuss how these findings illustrate how the SI Leader experience aligns with the characteristics of HIPs and confirm the findings of much of the existing literature on SI Leader experiences.

Demographics

SI Leaders represent a wide range of ages, class standings, majors, races, and ethnicities. The SI Leaders who responded to the ISPL-US reported a wide range of ages; however, the highest percentage (47.6%) of respondents reported that they were between 21 and 25 years old. There was also a wide range of class standing among SI Leaders in the sample, from first- to fifth-year students. Of the 123 SI Leaders who provided their major, most reported a major in the science, technology, engineering, and mathematics (STEM) field, whereas PLs in non-SI roles were much more likely to report a major in the social sciences. Interestingly, these results demonstrate a marked deviation from the beginnings of the SI program, when the UMKC initially offered SI mainly for graduate students in the Schools of Medicine, Dentistry, and Pharmacy (Martin & Arendale, 1992). Now, over 50 years later, SI both serves and employs undergraduate students.

Most SI Leaders in the ISPL survey identified as White (see Table 7.1). Except for those who identified as Asian or Asian American, very few SI Leaders in this survey hold a minoritized racial or ethnic identity. This trend is tremendously problematic and a key issue for SI program administrators to address. One possible barrier to participation as SI Leaders among students with minoritized identities may be the lack of representation in the faculty on college campuses. Faculty members play a key role in recommending students for SI Leader positions and serve a vital role in brokering these opportunities for students. Faculty members may be less likely to recognize students from underrepresented populations as potential SI Leaders. Relatedly, students with minoritized identities are less likely to seek out positions in which they do not see themselves represented.

Our analysis of the responses of SI Leaders also suggested that they were relatively financially privileged. While we are hesitant to make broad assumptions about the socioeconomic status of SI Leaders in the sample, we found it interesting that only 30.9% of SI Leaders indicated that they were eligible for federal financial aid through the Pell Grant program. Although this does not mean that the remaining 69.1% of SI Leaders do not have a need for financial aid, it points to the possibility of some degree of financial privilege among SI Leaders in the study.

Table 7.1

Race of SI Leaders Participating in 2023 ISPL-US

Race or ethnicity	SI Leaders ($n = 124$)		Total ($n = 1522$)	
	Freq.	%	Freq.	%
American Indian or Alaska Native	0	0.0	15	1.0
Asian or Asian American	27	21.8	134	8.8
Black or African American	2	1.6	107	7.0
Hispanic, Chicano/a, or Latino/a	14	11.3	229	15.0
Native Hawaiian or other Pacific Islander	1	0.8	13	0.9
White	84	67.7	1127	74.0
Other:	7	5.6	27	1.8
I prefer not to respond to this question	3	2.4	20	1.3

Training and Support

The extent of preparatory training afforded to the overall population of PLs in the 2023 ISPL-US exhibits notable variation; a small proportion of the overall population of PLs in the study (3.1%) expressed that they did not receive any form of initial training for their respective roles. In contrast, only 1.7% of SI Leaders indicated that they did not partake in any preparatory sessions or workshops. In general, nearly all PLs in the United States receive some sort of initial training, with SI Leaders even more likely to be receiving initial training. This underscores the significance of comprehensive onboarding and preparatory programs in equipping PLs with the essential skills and knowledge needed to excel in their positions.

In this study, SI Leaders reported receiving training ranging from just a few hours to three weeks, with the most common response being either two days (22%) or two weeks (22.9%). The Curators of the University of Missouri (2019) recommend in their supervisor training manual that programs, when able, offer a comprehensive two-day training. Over these two days, SI Leaders learn the program's history and foundation, best practices in planning and executing review sessions, and run through mock sessions.

In accordance with the recommendations of the ICSI, 82.2% of respondents reported that they received ongoing formal training following their initial training. Most frequently, SI Leaders indicated that their ongoing training occurred through regular training meetings. Other forms of ongoing training occurred through refresher sessions, retreats, staff meetings, meetings with the supervisor, and online or asynchronous self-paced training.

Support for SI Leaders is a key facet of the SI program, and the results of the ISPL-US demonstrate a high degree of fidelity to this essential program component. Indeed, 85% of SI Leader participants indicated that they had regular opportunities to receive feedback on their performance, compared to 74.7% of all surveyed PLs. Feedback on SI Leaders' performance came via student participant surveys and through meetings with supervising staff, faculty, or senior leaders. According to the survey, 84.2% of SI Leaders noted opportunities for reflection, compared to 73.2% of all PLs. This opportunity for reflection occurred most notably through group discussion with fellow SI Leaders at ongoing training sessions.

SI Leader Sense of Community

The ISCI emphasizes a structure of meaningful interaction with the campus community, including relationships between SI Leaders and faculty, staff, other PLs, and the students they serve. Not surprisingly, 57.5% of SI Leaders reported that they took on their role to become more involved in the university community. Excitingly, 47.9% of SI Leader survey respondents overwhelmingly noted that being a PL greatly increased their feelings of contributing to the community. This meaningful interaction with the campus community is also evident in the 82.9% of respondents sharing that their role had led to an increased sense of belonging at their institution.

Interactions with Peers

One of SI Leaders' primary responsibilities is to plan and execute study sessions for their peers. This involves significant amounts of time leading their peers in group study as part of formal SI sessions, as well as outreach to students to encourage their participation in SI sessions. The large amount of peer interaction associated with their role is evident in the fact that 98.3% of SI Leaders reported that being an SI Leader had led to an increase in meaningful interactions with their peers.

Additionally, a combined 87.1% of SI Leaders reported that their participation as a PL led to their increased interaction with people from different backgrounds (see Table 7.2), and 84.6% felt the role increased their knowledge about people with backgrounds different than their own (see Table 7.3).

Table 7.2

Reported Changes in Interactions with People from Different Backgrounds (*n* = 116)

	Freq.	%
Greatly decreased	0	0.0
Decreased	0	0.0
Slightly decreased	0	0.0
No change	13	11.2
Slightly increased	19	16.4
Increased	37	31.9
Greatly increased	45	38.8
Unable to judge	2	1.7

Table 7.3

Reported Changes in Knowledge About People from Different Backgrounds (*n* = 117)

	Freq.	%
Greatly decreased	0	0.0
Decreased	0	0.0
Slightly decreased	0	0.0
No change	16	13.7
Slightly increased	23	19.7
Increased	35	29.9
Greatly increased	41	35.0
Unable to judge	2	1.7

Interactions with Senior SI Leaders

SI Leaders also have the valuable chance to engage with another set of peers—their senior SI Leaders or mentors. More than half of SI Leaders in the survey reported that senior leaders were the source of their feedback and reflective opportunities. Specifically, 56.9% of SI Leader respondents reported receiving performance feedback from a senior leader within the program, in contrast to 36.2% of PLs in the overall ISPL-US sample. Additionally, they noted that 65.7% of their chances for reflection and integration stemmed from discussions with their senior PL, which was also significantly higher than the percentage of PLs in the overall sample who reported integrative learning opportunities facilitated by a senior PL (44.5%).

Interactions with Faculty and Staff

A substantial portion of an SI Leader's job responsibilities are associated with attending course lectures and meeting with faculty regularly throughout the semester. Accordingly, over 90% of SI Leaders indicated that their role as an SI Leader had increased their meaningful interactions with faculty members. This is a considerable strength of the SI model and sets it apart from other PL roles included in the ISPL-US, where only 76% of PLs reported that their PL experiences had led to an increase in their meaningful interactions with faculty. Past research provides convincing evidence for the strong connection between SI Leaders and the faculty members with whom they work. For example, Lockie and Van Lanen (2008) identified SI Leaders' relationships with faculty as an important theme of the SI Leader experience, where SI Leaders felt empowered to connect with faculty because of their on-campus role. In a later survey conducted by Lozada and Johnson (2018):

> Participants highlighted their increased comfort in their ability to talk one-on-one with faculty, which they attributed to the close faculty relationships they developed through the SI partnership, as well as in their ability to work with individuals different from themselves. (p. 103)

Table 7.4

Methods of Delivery for SI Leader Feedback (n = 102)

	Freq.	%
Meetings with a supervising faculty or staff member	77	75.5
Meetings with a senior PL	58	56.9
Surveys, questionnaires, or evaluations completed by the students who you led	46	45.1
As part of roleplay exercises, simulations, or mock teaching/advising sessions	29	28.4
Other	4	3.9

Over 90% of the SI Leaders surveyed also indicated that their role increased their meaningful interaction with staff, which would include their SI supervisor. Supervisors were the largest source of feedback for SI Leaders in the sample, with 75.5% reporting that they regularly received feedback through meetings with a supervising faculty or staff member (see Table 7.4). This is encouraging given that the ICSI regularly interacts with program supervisors through training sessions, webinars, and conferences to help them improve the support offered to SI Leaders. Additionally, these frequent interactions between supervisors and SI Leaders provide a forum in which SI Leaders can offer feedback to program administrators that helps improve the overall effectiveness of the SI program.

Stout and McDaniel (2006) further highlighted an added benefit that SI Leaders gain from serving in their role, namely recommendation letters. Through their role as an SI Leader, students can form meaningful relationships with the faculty and staff who can then provide personalized recommendation letters for the student and serve as genuine references. Accordingly, the SI Leader can use these connections for future opportunities and, we hypothesize, upward mobility. This is an exciting potential phenomenon to explore in future research on peer leadership.

Impact on Supplemental Instruction Leader Development

The ISPL-US also gathered data regarding the impact that being an SI Leader had on the following skills: academic, critical thinking, time management, organizational, project management, leadership, teamwork and collaboration, interpersonal communication, written communication, presentation, problem-solving, decision-making, adaptability, and creativity. SI Leaders reported the most significant gains in their leadership, adaptability, and presentation skills. Additionally, nearly 60% of SI Leaders reported that their SI Leader experiences increased their chances of success in obtaining a full-time job following their graduation. This result is surprisingly lower than similar survey findings from Malm et al. (2022), which found that 82% of SI Leaders at UMKC believed that serving in their role had a positive impact on their post-graduate employability.

Leadership

Past research has linked the PL experience to the improvement of leadership skills (Congos & Stout, 2003; James & Moore, 2018 Lozada, 2017; Malm et al., 2022; Stout & McDaniel, 2006). This was true for the results of the ISPL-US study with 59.8% of SI Leaders indicating that participating as a PL greatly increased their leadership skills. Complementing direct leadership skills, 87.2% of SI Leaders felt their teamwork and collaboration skills increased, and 86.3% felt their decision-making skills increased. Given the collaborative and relational nature of the work that SI Leaders engage in, it should not be surprising that SI Leaders report significant gains in their abilities related to teamwork and collaboration.

Adaptability

SI Leaders also indicated that being a PL greatly increased their adaptability skills. Indeed, the pre-term and ongoing training provided to SI Leaders emphasizes the importance of adaptability in sessions. Leaders must be able to adapt their session plans to account for actual attendance in the session, the current knowledge level of attendees, and the availability of resources. For instance, if an SI Leader intends on having small groups work together for an activity during the session but only has two attendees, the SI Leader must be able to alter the planned activity to work for those students.

Ghio et al. correctly highlighted the fact that SI Leaders have an opportunity to "take on leadership roles that introduce them to challenges they likely would not face during regular coursework" (2020, p.3). While the SI Leader would have an instructor, teaching assistant, or tutor to turn to for their regular coursework, they are unable to do so in their SI sessions. Instead, they must be able to think quickly and modify their session plan in the moment.

Presentation Skills

Significantly, 42.2% of SI Leaders indicated that being a PL greatly increased their presentation skills, compared to the 28.2% of overall PL respondents. This is by no means a surprise, as the SI model requires SI Leaders to regularly facilitate group discussions and prioritizes building confidence and public speaking skills. Congos and Stout (2003) accurately pointed out that "[i]n a 15-week semester where an SI Leader offers three SI sessions per week, there are 45 hours of time in which to practice communication skills and build confidence often with observation and feedback from an SI supervisor" (p. 33). In addition to their review sessions, SI Leaders can improve their presentation skills through ongoing training activities, feedback from supervisors and senior leaders, and reflection on their practice. These skills can increase even more for SI Leaders who move into a senior leadership role within their program.

Again, the results of the ISPL-US for SI Leaders provide robust evidence of its alignment with the characteristics of HIPs: high expectations, meaningful interactions with faculty and peers, opportunities for feedback and reflection, and public demonstration of learning. Additionally, the structure of SI—wherein SI

Leaders occupy a liminal space that allows them to both facilitate learning for less experienced peers and learn from more senior peers and supervisors—is a powerful example of how peer leadership embodies *legitimate peripheral participation* (Lave & Wenger, 1991). This discussion has also illustrated how the SI model leverages the modes of transition (Young & Bunting, 2024)—*community, participation,* and *becoming*—to provide highly impactful experiences for SI Leaders.

Practical Guidance and Recommendations

As highlighted above, the results of the ISPL-US survey revealed many areas in which students currently serving as SI Leaders reported meaningful growth. However, there were a number of areas in which reported gains were much more modest. It is prudent to take note of these areas and make necessary adaptations to SI programming to better support SI Leaders in growing in these additional areas.

Career Readiness

While we did see roughly 60% of respondents agree to the impact the role of SI Leader could have on their post-graduate employability, there were 18.9% of respondents who saw their role as SI Leader having no impact on their potential to succeed in a career after graduation and an additional 21.6% shared that they were unable to judge the impact the role could have on their career readiness. Administrators of SI programs could address this gap through a renewed focus on both SI Leader recruitment and training.

Supplemental Instruction Leader Recruitment Process

Although not directly addressed in the ISPL-US instrument, we consistently hear from institutions who are struggling with the recruitment of new SI Leaders. The survey data related to the degree to which SI Leaders believe their PL experiences are preparing them for future employability suggest that prospective SI Leaders may not fully understand the potential that the SI Leader experience has to equip them with important employability skills. The ICSI recommends that program administrators emphasize career readiness throughout recruiting SI Leaders and highlight the unique benefits of being an SI Leader.

One way we recommend that programs can accomplish this is to have a robust feedback loop with SI Leader alumni able to tell their stories to prospective SI Leaders. This could include sharing testimonials from alumni in various fields with students enrolled in high-risk courses where there is a desire for increased SI Leader involvement. Allowing students to see the impact serving as an SI Leader can have on post-graduation opportunities is likely to increase attraction of these roles and result in more effective SI Leader recruitment for institutions hoping to increase interest in the SI Leader role.

Training Emphasis

More intentional support and training around the connection between the work done in the SI Leader role and the work that SI Leaders hope to do upon the completion of their degree is another way to improve employability outcomes among SI Leaders. For instance, UMKC requires SI Leaders to engage in a 360-review process throughout every term they serve in the role. This process brings in data from their observations, student evaluations, and peer evaluations, to help them develop their skills. The process also includes three check-in meetings with their supervisor to discuss their goals inside and outside of their SI sessions. These meetings provide a powerful reflective space where SI Leaders can articulate longer term personal career goals and consider how their SI work can help them achieve those goals. Additionally, the ICSI also encourages programs to cover topics such as resume building and interviewing skills in ongoing training sessions to help SI Leaders learn to articulate their experiences in a meaningful way. Though not directly related to the work SI Leaders do in their sessions, these trainings are essential in helping SI Leaders recognize the opportunities for career development that are inherent in their work.

Unanswered Questions/Directions for Future Research

As we reviewed the literature related to the findings of the ISPL-US, we observed a lack of research specifically on qualitative aspects of the SI Leader experience in contexts in the United States. Our partners in the ICSI are continuing to conduct research in this area, but there is a great deal of work left for us to do in the United States. Below, we recommend additional research that could be beneficial regarding how the SI Leaders learn and grow in their position.

Programs' Experience with the International Center for Supplemental Instruction

The ICSI offers a wide range of professional development opportunities for the professional staff and faculty that work with SI Leaders at their given institutions. It is unclear from the ISPL-US what level of professional development supervisors had received and how this might have impacted outcomes among SI Leader respondents. Also, it is unclear if the SI Leaders surveyed were from accredited SI programs. It would be beneficial for the ICSI to conduct a similar research study across accredited programs to gain a clearer picture of the impact of the accreditation standards on SI Leader growth and development.

Modality and Topics of Training

Training is a vital part of any PL's experience; however, there are some lingering questions left about training delivery and the topics covered in training. It is difficult to glean from this study whether the benefits reported by those surveyed were simply from their experience in doing the work, or whether the benefits came because the training they received addressed these topics. For instance, written communication is a huge component of an SI Leader's job responsibility and yet over 30% of SI Leaders surveyed reported no change to their written communication in association with their PL role.

Additionally, approximately 30% of respondents reported receiving online, self-paced training. Future research could explore the perceived effectiveness of this training modality for their role and which topics the training addressed in this modality. This information could be helpful to programs looking to adapt their current training protocols to prepare PLs to function in online settings and to address some of the post-pandemic needs of our student leader population.

Feedback

As we have discussed in this chapter, feedback is essential in supporting our SI Leaders and providing them with opportunities for growth. While results of the ISPL-US provided evidence that SI Leaders "regularly received feedback" and offered insight into the mechanisms through which SI Leaders received feedback, future research should explore *how often* SI Leaders have opportunities for feedback and *for what* aspects of their role they receive feedback. As discussed previously, SI Leaders typically receive feedback through observations and student evaluations, but programs could also look for ways to offer feedback to SI Leaders related to administrative tasks such as the promotional emails they send to students or the planning sheets they turn in.

In general, the ICSI recommends that new SI Leaders receive feedback via observations eight times and that returning SI Leaders receive feedback 10 times each semester. We recognize that programs may face limitations in providing feedback based on a lack of time, resources, or personnel. For example, if an SI program has 40 SI Leaders but only one supervisor and a small number of senior PLs, it may be impossible to conduct enough observations to meet ICSI's recommendations. In these cases, we recommend that programs assess the areas in which feedback can be most useful.

Benefits Among Senior Peer Leaders

Although the ISPL-US Survey addresses SI Leader interactions with other peers, staff members, and faculty, little is known about the unique experiences of those who serve in senior PL positions. Senior SI Leaders play a significant role by providing additional support to new SI Leaders, assisting in session planning, and conducting ongoing training sessions throughout the semester. Future research could examine how experiences as a senior leader impact the growth and learning reported by PLs.

Conclusion

Our journeys both began with our roles as SI Leaders at our individual universities; therefore, it is fitting for this chapter to conclude with a reflection of how the benefits observed in this survey manifested in our cases.

Jessica Pearson

I currently serve as the Executive Director of the International Center for Supplemental Instruction, a role that would be impossible if not for my experience as an SI Leader at Florida Atlantic University for a majority of my undergraduate career. The biggest impact for me came from the meaningful relationships with faculty, staff, and peers that my role as an SI Leader afforded me on campus. I was a commuter student, and prior to my role as SI Leader, my life on campus consisted of going to class and hanging out in my car waiting for my next class to start. Once I joined the SI team, I found a community to belong to on campus. The relationships I developed and interactions I had with both the students who attended my sessions and the supervisors who mentored me directly contributed to completing my degree. They also launched me onto my future career path into higher education.

Kate Verheyn

I began as an SI Leader for World History in the fall semester of 2019 at the University of West Georgia. The results of the ISPL survey highlighted in this chapter align with my own experiences as an SI Leader. While I had little work experience when I began, I worked with faculty members and a supervisor who invested in me for four semesters. The ongoing training sessions that covered topics such as professionalism, leadership skills, communication, and time management were particularly impactful. Combined with the ongoing feedback I received from the staff members and graduate students who supervised me, I grew into an outgoing and well-prepared SI Leader. After graduating, I returned to campus as the Graduate Assistant for Supplemental Instruction and later transitioned into the role of Coordinator of Supplemental Instruction.

The 2023 ISPL-US reflects much of what we have seen in our direct experiences and through reviewing the existing literature: SI Leaders experience tremendous benefits from their experience in this role. Through serving as a PL in an SI program, SI Leaders develop their skills in leadership, adaptability, collaboration, and presentation. They build valuable networks with their faculty members, the programmatic staff members who supervise them, and their fellow peers, including other SI Leaders and the students enrolled in the class. As SI Leaders transition from their role as an undergraduate student to their role in a professional field upon graduation, their experiences as an SI Leader can provide them with immense opportunities for success.

References

Burmeister, S., & Martin, D. (1996). Supplemental instruction: An interview with Deanna Martin. *Journal of Developmental Education, 20*(1), 22-26.

Congos, D., & Stout, B. (2003). The benefits of SI leadership after graduation. *Research and Teaching in Developmental Education, 20*(1), 29-41. http://www.jstor.org/stable/42802548

Curators of the University of Missouri. (2019). *Supervisor manual.* [Handbook]. University of Missouri-Kansas City.

Ghio, C., Morris, S. A., Boyce, H. M., Priem, B. J., DiMilla, P., & Reisberg, R. (2020). *The impacts of peer tutors of leading group supplemental instruction for first-year engineering students.* ASEE Virtual Conference. http://dx.doi.org/10.18260/1-2--35336

Hoiland, S. L., Reyes, S., & Varelas, A. (2020). The impact of a supplemental instruction program on diverse peer leaders at a two-year institution. *Journal of Peer Learning, 13*, 5-20.

Hurley, M., Jacobs, G., & Gilbert, M. (2006). The basic SI model. *New Directions for Teaching and Learning, 2006*(106), 11–22. https://doi.org/10.1002/tl.229

James, A., & Moore, L. (2018). Understanding the supplemental instruction leader. *Learning Assistance Review, 23*(1), 9–29. https://eric.ed.gov/?id=EJ1170156

Kuh, G. D., & O'Donnell, K. (2013). *Ensuring quality and taking high-impact practices to scale.* American Association of Colleges and Universities.

Lave, J., & Wenger, E. (1991). *Situated learning: Legitimate peripheral participation.* Cambridge University Press. https://psycnet.apa.org/doi/10.1017/CBO9780511815355

Lockie, N. M., & Van Lanen, R. J. (2008). Impact of the supplemental instruction experience on science SI leaders. *Journal of Developmental Education, 31*(3), 2-12.

Lozada, N. (2017). The benefits of supplemental instruction (SI) for the SI leader. *Supplemental Instruction Journal, 3*(1), 64–79.

Lozada, N., & Johnson, A. T. (2018). Bridging the supplemental instruction leader experience and post-graduation life. *Learning Assistance Review, 23*(1), 95–114.

Malm, J., Collins, J., Nel, C., Smith, L., Carey, W., Miller, H., Khagram, K., & Zaccagnini, M. (2022). Transferable skills gained by student leaders in international SI-pass programs. *The International Journal of Learning in Higher Education, 29*(1), 65–82. https://doi.org/10.18848/2327-7955/CGP/v29i01/65-82

Martin, D. C., & Arendale, D. R. (Eds.). (1992). *Supplemental instruction: Improving first-year student success in high-risk courses* (2nd ed.). Monograph Series No. 7. University of South Carolina, National Resource Center for The First Year Experience and Students in Transition. Available online: ERIC database (ED354839).

Stout, M. L., & McDaniel, A. J. (2006). Benefits to supplemental instruction leaders. *New Directions for Teaching and Learning, 2006*(106), 55–62. https://doi.org/10.1002/tl.233

Young, D. G., & Bunting, B. D. (2024). Rethinking college transitions: Legitimate peripheral participation as a pathway to becoming. *AERA Open, 10,* https://doi.org/10.1177/23328584241255631.

Chapter 8

Peer Leadership and Sense of Belonging in Campus Activities

Sarah Keeling
National Association for Campus Activities

The National Association for Campus Activities (NACA) posits that the core purpose of Campus Activities is to create a sense of belonging. While activities traditionally viewed as peer leadership, such as tutoring or peer mentoring, may not be typically considered as Campus Activities, peer leadership occurs daily in student organizations, event planning and implementation, and everyday interactions among activities staff. Thus, Campus Activities have the potential to impact the sense of belonging of peer leaders (PLs) in important ways. NACA defines sense of belonging as "the extent to which individuals feel their authentic self is personally accepted, respected, included, supported, and safe in the university environment" (2023a, para. 5). This feeling is influenced by factors such as involvement on campus, relationships with peers and educators, and academic integration (Vaccaro & Newman, 2022).

NACA defines Campus Activities as "beyond-the-classroom experiences that intentionally connect, engage, and develop a college community where everyone belongs" (2023a, para. 2). The purpose of Campus Activities is to "create strategies for deeply engaging students with each other and to connect them with the institutions" they attend (Peck et al., 2020, p. 5). This engagement not only benefits the institution, but, more importantly, student participants develop important skills, particularly in terms of employability (Peck et al., 2020). The 2023 International Survey of Peer Leaders-US (ISPL-US) defined PLs as students selected to serve as mentors, advisors, or educators of other students through a campus-run organization. In terms of gains in sense of belonging related to PL experiences, van der Meer et al. (2019) found that PLs do indeed strengthen their sense of belonging as they are provided with opportunities to contribute to their campus community.

In this chapter, I will discuss key findings related to Campus Activities PLs who participated in the ISPL-US study. Specifically, I will discuss how these findings provide support for the argument made by van der Meer et al. (2022) that peer leadership experiences do indeed contribute to PLs' sense of belonging.

A Brief Review of the Literature on Sense of Belonging, Campus Activities, and Peer Leadership

While there are a host of factors that contribute to college students' sense of belonging, past research has provided evidence that "what students *do* during college counts more for what they learn and whether they will persist in college" (Kuh et al., 2005, p. 8). Indeed, research on student success has long shown that involvement and engagement in Campus Activities leads to retention and persistence. For example, Tinto's (1987) Model of Institutional Departure outlined that "experiences, academic and social, which serve to integrate the individual into the life of the college, also serve to heighten attachments and therefore strengthen individual commitments both to the goal of education and to the institution" (p. 5). Similarly, Komives (2019) discussed research around Campus Activities and how degree completion was positively impacted when participating in Campus

Activities. Ultimately, Campus Activities are transformative because they provide students opportunities to "develop, grow and learn" (Dungy & Peck, 2019, p. 7), and create a sense of belonging for students within their campus community.

While sense of belonging is a feeling within an individual, it involves more than that one person; it involves a community. Based in Durkheim's work on the nature of belonging, Nunn (2021) argued that belonging is bestowed (or not) by other community members and that to experience true belonging they must feel that they belong to the wider campus community. A student may feel that they belong to a specific student organization and still not feel that they belong on their campus (Nunn, 2021).

In Nunn's (2021) study of first-year and first-generation students, participants differentiated between social belonging, campus-community belonging, and academic belonging. Further, Nunn (2021) makes a compelling case for the need to attend, holistically, to all three of these domains of belonging, pointing out that campus-community belonging is often neglected:

> No matter how well we do as a university in linking students to resource centers, student organizations, sports teams, academic clubs, friendships, academic mentorships, and so on, we cannot count ourselves successful until we are also offering the gift of belonging to our students at the campus-community level at the same time. Of course, this is a much more challenging task than creating a space or program in which students can feel supported, valued, and "at home." It requires shifts in the broader campus culture. (p. 11)

Strayhorn (2022) echoed this need to attend to campus-community belonging, stating that focusing only on simplistic notions of belonging between individual students "ignores or downplays the critical role that institutions and actors can play in successful navigation" (p. 28) of the institution. PLs in Campus Activities play a key role in these institutional efforts by mentoring their peers in Campus Activities, serving as officers for a campus organization, and providing organizational training (Cuseo, 2007).

Campus Activities Peer Leader Outcomes Related to Sense of Belonging

Several items in the ISPL-US instrument were aimed at providing understanding of how participants' peer leadership experiences influenced their sense of belonging. Of the respondents serving in Campus Activities PL roles, 86.8% indicated that, as a direct result of their peer leadership experience, their feeling of belonging and welcome at their institution increased (12.2% slightly increased, 27.9% increased, 46.7% greatly increased). Additionally, Campus Activities PLs were much more likely to have reported that their PL experiences "greatly increased" their feelings of that they belong and are welcome on their campus (47.6%) than were the overall sample of respondents (37.8%).

Respondents also indicated that their desire to stay at their institution and graduate increased (9.1% slightly increased, 25.8% increased, 48.5% greatly increased) due to their Campus Activities PL experience. Again, the percentage of Campus Activities PLs who reported that their desire to stay and graduate had "greatly increased" (48.5%) was noticeably higher than for overall respondents (34.9%).

Finally, over 90% of PLs in Campus Activities reported increases in feeling they were contributing to the campus community (6.6% slightly increased, 34.3% increased, 52% greatly increased). Thus, overall, Campus Activities PLs who participated in the ISPL-US seemed to believe that their PL experiences had made a significant impact on their sense of belonging on their campus. This aligns with the work of Vaccaro and Newman (2022) that found that sense of belonging is influenced by factors such as relationships with peers and educators, involvement on campus, and "a need to master the student role and achieve academic success" (p. 9). Campus Activities seems to provide PLs with opportunities to form these relationships, be involved in meaningful ways, and develop both academic and social skills. In short, my analysis of the ISPL-US data for Campus Activities PLs provided evidence that this group of PLs were experiencing all three types of the belonging described by Nunn (2021). In the following discussion, I explore how the results of the ISPL-US for Campus Activities PLs provide insight into the impact that being a PL can have on each of these domains of belonging.

Relationships and Social Belonging

Astin (1993) stated that students' peer group has a larger impact on their growth and development than nearly any other aspect of their experience. As discussed in Chapter 2 of this report, for participants in the ISPL-US, serving as a PL had a powerful impact on their relationships with peers. This aligns with the findings of a study conducted by Colvin and Ashman (2010) where PLs reported that interacting with others and developing friendships was one of the most pronounced benefits of being a PL. Similarly, Ellison and Braxton (2022) posited that social interactions like those experienced by PLs contribute to what they termed a *peer-anchored sense of belonging.*

For Campus Activities PLs who participated in the study, their greatest reported gains in sense of social belonging were associated with relationships with peers (see Table 8.1), where 11.2% indicated that their "meaningful interactions with peers" had slightly increased; 37.1% reported that they had "increased," and 46.2% reported that their meaningful interactions with peers had "greatly increased," which was noticeably higher than the percentage of overall respondents who reported that their meaningful interactions with peers had greatly increased (41.1%).

Table 8.1

The Degree to Which Campus Activities PLs' Social Belonging Greatly Increased as a Result of Their Experiences

	Campus Activities respondents			All respondents		
	N	Freq.	%	N	Freq.	%
Meaningful interaction with peers	197	91	46.2	1276	525	41.1
Meaningful interaction with staff members	197	83	42.1	1293	413	31.9
Meaningful interaction with faculty	198	75	37.9	1295	366	28.3
Build relationships with people with whom you work	191	83	43.5	1263	510	40.4

There was an even greater difference between PLs in Campus Activities and all ISPL-US respondents with regard to their meaningful interactions with staff members. Just over 42% of PLs in Campus Activities said their meaningful interactions with staff members had "greatly increased" because of their peer leadership experience, which was over 10 percentage points higher than for the overall sample of PLs in the study (31.9%). I observed a similar trend related to participants' meaningful interactions with faculty. Just over 28% of the total ISPL-US sample said their meaningful interactions with faculty greatly increased, while 37.9 % of PLs in Campus Activities reported that their meaningful interactions with faculty had greatly increased as a result of their PL experiences.

Finally, Campus Activities respondents were more likely to report that their ability to build relationships with the people with whom they work had increased through their experiences, than were the overall group of respondents. Though ISPL-US results do not provide clear understanding of why Campus Activities PLs were more likely to report that their PL experiences greatly increased the interactions they had with peers, faculty, and staff, we hypothesize that this is due to the structure of the Campus Activities PL experience. Because of the nature of their role, Campus Activities PLs spend significant amounts of time meeting regularly with faculty or staff advisors and participating alongside faculty, staff, and peers in activities. Consequently, there are abundant opportunities for these PLs to interact with their peers, supervising staff, and faculty in meaningful ways related to the tasks of their role. This is an important finding given that interactions with faculty, staff, and peers around important matters are a characteristic of high-impact practices (HIPs) and contribute to meaningful learning gains for students, particularly those on the margins (Teaching & Learning Resource Center, n.d.). Additionally, Dias (2022) found that relationships established with peers were crucial to feeling integrated onto campus. Thus, PLs in Campus Activities roles have the potential to experience significant gains in their sense of social belonging.

Involvement in Campus Activities and Campus-Community Belonging

The ISPL-US also allows us to explore how Campus Activities PLs' experiences foster their involvement on campus and the degree to which they are experiencing the campus-community belonging described by Lisa Nunn (2021). Astin (1999) described student involvement in this way:

> Quite simply, student involvement refers to the amount of physical and psychological energy that the student devotes to the academic experience. Thus, a highly involved student is one who, for example, devotes considerable energy to studying, spends much time on campus, participates actively in student organizations, and interacts frequently with faculty members and other students. (p. 518)

Similarly, in a study conducted by Duerr (2020), students described involvement as activities that gave them a sense of purpose and community, such as being a member of a club. For Campus Activities PLs in the ISPL-US their experiences contributed to these feelings of belonging to the broader campus community.

PLs in Campus Activities who participated in the ISPL-US were more likely than other participants in the study to have held more than one PL position. When asked how many total PL positions they held during their university experience, 74.1% of Campus Activities PLs stated they held between two to six positions, while only 58.1% of overall participants reported holding two to six positions during college. Additionally, Campus Activities PLs were more likely to have served in a senior PL role (52.2%) than the overall group of participants in the study (35.7%). This aligns with the work of Loper (2022) that demonstrated a clear connection between sense of belonging and involvement in a student organization or beyond-the-classroom campus activity.

ISPL-US results do not offer clear understanding of why Campus Activities PLs are more likely to be involved in multiple PL experiences, or why they tend to have senior PL opportunities at a greater rate than other PLs; however, this is an area ripe with opportunities for future research.

Campus Activities PLs' Academic Integration and Academic Belonging

Tinto (1997) posited that the classroom is central to college communities and is a "major feature" of every student's educational experience (p. 599). Vaccaro and Newman (2022) stated that students' sense of belonging grows as they "achieve academic success" (p. 4) and excel in their role as a student. Similarly, Tinto stated:

> Students with a sense of belonging in academic settings feel socially connected, supported, and respected by others, including peers, faculty/teachers, and administrators. They trust their teachers and peers generally and, consequently, feel a sense of fit at school. They are not worried about being treated like a stereotype or "less than" and, thus, are confident that they are seen (visible), cared about, and a person of worth who adds value to the academic learning space… (as cited in Strayhorn, 2022, pp. 27-28)

The current study asked PLs about 14 different skills that can be tied to academic integration and academic belonging. PLs in Campus Activities saw the greatest gains in academic skill development in project management, leadership, problem solving, teamwork and collaboration (see Table 8.2).

Handy (2017) found that leadership skills are positively associated with GPA. Similarly, Stadler et al. (2015) stated that problem solving skills are strongly correlated with academic success and GPA. Based on the results of the ISPL-US, PLs in Campus Activities roles are growing in these ways. Consequently, we can surmise that experiences as a Campus Activities PL are contributing to students' academic confidence and sense of academic belonging. However, over 63% of the Campus Activities respondents (63.8%) reported a GPA of 3.50 to 4.00, which is lower than the percentage of participants in the overall ISPL-US sample who reported a GPA in this upper range. Thus, Campus Activities staff should continue to look for ways to intentionally structure Campus

Activities PL experiences in ways that contribute to essential academic skills and position Campus Activities PLs for academic success.

Table 8.2

"Greatly Increased" Academic Skill as a Result of Peer Leadership

Skill	PLs in Campus Activities			Total respondents		
	N	Freq.	%	N	Freq.	%
Leadership	196	120	61.2	1288	684	53.1
Teamwork & collaboration	195	93	47.7	1288	527	40.9
Interpersonal communication	195	91	46.7	1287	562	43.7
Adaptability	199	92	46.2	1300	541	41.6
Project management	195	77	39.5	1287	398	30.9
Time management	192	72	37.5	1282	502	39.2
Problem solving	199	73	36.7	1294	383	29.6
Organizational	195	71	36.4	1290	438	34.0
Decision making	198	68	34.3	1294	402	31.1
Presentation	198	65	32.8	1289	363	28.2
Critical thinking	199	65	32.7	1304	366	28.1
Creativity	199	64	32.2	1305	341	26.1
Written communication	196	44	22.4	1293	279	21.6
General academic abilities	199	34	17.1	1303	200	15.3

Discussion and Implications

A little over 15% of respondents to the ISPL-US indicated that they were PLs within Campus Activities. Only six of those students, or 2.8% of Campus Activities PLs, indicated that they were first-year students, which is nearly half the percentage of respondents in the overall sample who indicated that they were first-year students. Among Campus Activities PLs, 30% reported that they were second-year students and 28% that they were third-year students. The percentage of fourth-year Campus Activities PLs (30.8%) was also higher than the percentage of fourth-year PLs in the overall sample (25.7%; see Table 8.3). Based on these data, it appears that Campus Activities PLs are, on average, further along in their college experience.

While this may be due, in part, to position requirements that dictate that Campus Activities PLs have some degree of prior experience on campus, this can also serve as a problematic barrier to entry. Those who administer Campus Activities programs should consider how novice students might be invited and encouraged to participate in developmentally appropriate PL roles that do not require deep experience. Doing so will not only offer opportunities for participation to additional students, involving students in Campus Activities PL roles earlier in their experience will also provide a stronger pool of applicants for more advanced Campus Activities PL roles. Lave and Wenger's (1991) conceptualization of *legitimate peripheral participation* offers a theory-based rationale for this approach and suggests that the sooner novice participants can be brought into meaningful interaction with more knowledgeable others in their communities (e.g., more experienced Campus Activities PLs, staff supervisors), the more likely they will be to develop essential skills and abilities and to feel like contributing members of their community.

Overall, the ISPL-US data clearly illustrate the impact that peer leadership in Campus Activities has on sense of belonging for PLs. This is especially important when we consider the demographics of the Campus Activities PLs. In general, these students were more racially and ethnically diverse, more likely to be first-generation students, and more were eligible for Pell Grants. For students who view themselves on the margins of the campus community or who are perceived as such by the institution, sense of belonging is especially important (Strayhorn, 2019). A 2020 study showed that underrepresented racial-ethnic minorities (URM) and first-generation students "at 4-year colleges reported lower belonging than their peers" (Gopalan & Brady, p. 3). Literature around this topic shows that students with a lower socioeconomic status experience less feelings of belonging on campus (Ellison & Braxton, 2022). These students often must work more than their peers and have less time and capacity to get engaged on campus. However, the increases in sense of belonging and skill development for PLs in Campus Activities were greater than the average ISPL-US respondent. This illustrates that Campus Activities helps these students find their place with their campus community.

Analysis of the data for Campus Activities PLs in the ISPL-US also revealed an interesting pattern related to the demographic profile of Campus Activities PLs, particularly in comparison to the overall sample of PLs who participated in the ISPL. For example, Campus Activities PLs in the study were less likely to have reported that at least one of their parents earned a four-year degree (73% of Campus Activities respondents; 75.8% total respondents) and were more likely to have reported that they were eligible for financial aid under the Pell Grant program (37.4% of Campus Activities respondents; 31.2% total respondents). Additionally, Campus Activities respondents were more racially, ethnically, and socio-economically diverse than the overall group of respondents (see Table 8.3). Just under 70% of the students were White (compared to 74% total); 15.6% Hispanic, Chicano/a, or Latino/a (compared to 15% total); and 14.2% Black or African American (compared to 7%).

Table 8.3

Demographic Profile of Campus Activities Leaders

	Campus Activities respondents			Total respondents		
	N	Freq.	%	N	Freq.	%
Fourth-year student	211	65	30.8	1531	394	25.7
GPA of 3.5-4.0	207	132	63.8	1483	1055	71.1
Parents with a 4-year degree	211	154	73.0	1529	1159	75.8
Pell Grant eligible	211	79	37.4	1528	476	31.2
White	211	141	66.8	1522	1127	74.0

These data suggest that, for reasons not explored in the ISPL-US, first-generation students, Pell-eligible students, and Students of Color appear to be more likely to end up in Campus Activities PL roles than the other PL roles included in the survey. This is a tremendously important pattern to note. Again, it is not clear from the ISPL-US data what might explain these differences. Possibilities include identity-based and identity-conscious Campus Activities organizations that have well-designed marketing and recruitment strategies, or Campus Activities professionals who create more welcoming environments for students from underrepresented populations. Scholars in this space should conduct future research to provide clearer understanding of who ends up in Campus Activities PL roles, why marginalized students seem to be overrepresented in these roles, and what can be done to leverage Campus Activities as a fruitful space for contributing to the broader work of increasing access and equity on college campuses.

The field of Campus Activities is uniquely positioned to offer transformational educational experiences for students who may be on the margins at their institutions. The data from this study showed that PLs in Campus Activities developed a sense of belonging and academic-related skills at a higher rate than did the overall survey sample. This negates the sometime held belief that Campus Activities are simply about fun, which can lead to reduced funding and staffing (Peck et al, 2020).

Recommendations

The first recommendation is to incorporate the NACA Student Leadership Competencies into PL training and development (NACA, 2023b). The NACA Student Leadership Competencies are designed to be a tool for advisors who work with PLs in Campus Activities contexts. They provide a framework for advisors to use to help students articulate the employability, leadership, and soft skills students gain through campus engagement. The competencies consist of four domain areas: (a) Programming, (b) Organization Development, (c) Individual Leadership Development, and (d) Diversity, Equity, Inclusion & Accessibility. Each domain is broken into tasks and competencies that can help students gain aptitude in that area (NACA, 2023b). The document also outlines suggestions for incorporating the competencies into PL training, student organization meetings, or PL reflections.

Second, PLs in Campus Activities may not consider themselves to be PLs because peer leadership may typically be viewed as related to academics (such as academic coaches and supplemental instructors). Students who are leaders within student organizations may not fully understand that they are not just organizing activities, but that they are serving as leaders, mentors, and models to the students who participate in and contribute to these activities. Professional staff and advisors should be sure to emphasize that Campus Activities do not just engage students in enjoyable events, but that they have a significant impact on the growth and development of those who organize and lead these activities. Professional staff and advisors can help PLs reflect on, identify, and articulate the employability and soft skills they gain from serving as a PL.

One helpful tool for facilitating this learning is the NACA Employability Skills Assessment (2023c). This tool incorporates the National Association for Colleges and Employers (NACE) competencies for career readiness and outlines the employability skills that employers are seeking. The NACA Employability Skills Assessment (NACA, 2023c) allows students to reflect on their involvement and evaluate the degree to which their involvement in Campus Activities has helped them develop core employability skills. Campus Activities advisors can engage in reflective dialogue with PLs to further deepen the learning that results from engaging with the assessment and to support Campus Activities PLs in outlining paths toward future growth and development. Interactions like this are excellent examples of how Campus Activities PLs can be provided with high-impact experiences that offer meaningful interactions with faculty and staff, offer powerful opportunities for reflection, and that support PLs in integrating and applying their learning in real-world contexts.

Third, Campus Activities administrators should employ strategies to continue to extend PL opportunities to students from underrepresented populations. To engage underrepresented racial–ethnic minorities, Museus et al. (2020) have offered numerous approaches, including examining institutional and programmatic mission statements, fostering peer networks, supporting culturally focused organizations and spaces, and providing professional development for student leaders. Providing physical spaces, such as an office or lounge, and figurative spaces, such as student organizations, for students who are not widely represented on campus, can help them to connect and increase their sense of belonging. Training PLs on how to engage, work, and have difficult conversations with students from a variety of backgrounds can help "promote inclusion and racial interactions across their organizations" (Museus et al., 2020, p. 29).

Similarly, efforts should be made to extend Campus Activities PL opportunities to increasing numbers of first-generation students. Kouzoukas (2020) has wisely suggested that "instead of creating programs for first-generation students, create programs with them" (p. 301). This approach of involving first-generation students as co-participants in the creation of campus activities is an excellent example of *legitimate peripheral participation* (Lave & Wenger, 1991), and honors the expertise that students bring with them to college and invites them to participate alongside administrators to help design more effective campus programming.

Social class and socioeconomic status are often overlooked in relation to the PL experience. For example, nearly half of the Campus Activities PLs in the study reported that they were volunteers and did not receive any compensation for their work. When PL roles are uncompensated, they become very inaccessible to low-income students, adult learners with family obligations, and others with financial need. Professional staff and advisors who work with Campus Activities PLs need to work to explore ways to compensate these students whenever possible.

Ardoin (2020) has outlined several strategies to engage and support working class students. Though her research did not focus specifically on PLs or Campus Activities, these strategies can be adapted for application in Campus Activities contexts, where working class students seem to be overrepresented. First, work to raise the consciousness of faculty, staff, and administration associated with Campus Activities around social class identity. Assisting these students can include finding ways to connect poor and working-class students to paid Campus Activity positions fellow students and faculty/staff on campus. Additionally, Campus Activities staff should carefully consider what additional hidden costs to being a PL might be present in terms of time requirements, schedules that require work during mealtimes but that do not include meals, and so on.

Fourth, Campus Activities leaders should continue to align the campus activities PL experience with the characteristics of HIPs, by building frequent opportunities for reflection and integration of learning, supporting Campus Activities PLs in applying their learning in contexts outside their specific job responsibilities, and providing meaningful opportunities for PLs to share their learning and demonstrate their competence. Consider implementing a high impact practice, such as a reflection portfolio or some sort of capstone project, so students have a structured opportunity to reflect on their time and work and articulate how their experiences have prepared them for future roles. Again, the NACA Student Leadership Competencies (2023b) and the NACA Employability Skills Assessment (2023c) can be valuable tools in these efforts.

Finally, gathering personal stories from Campus Activities PLs that demonstrate how they have grown and what they have learned—particularly with regard to their sense of belonging and future employability—can be invaluable in recruitment efforts and demonstrating to institutional leaders the powerful impact that Campus Activities peer leadership can have in contributing to students' sense of belonging and retention and persistence on campus. Similarly, seasoned Campus Activities PLs can serve as ambassadors on campus by being invited to share their stories of growth and development and the importance of Campus Activities to a campus community. Peer leadership in Campus Activities has a powerful story to tell. Go tell it.

References

Ardoin, S. (2020). Engaging poor and working-class students. In S. J. Quaye, S. R. Harper, & S. L. Pendakur (Eds.), *Student engagement in higher education: Theoretical perspectives and practical approaches for diverse populations* (pp. 307-323). Routledge.

Astin, A. W. (1993). *What matters in college? Four critical years revisited.* Jossey-Bass.

Astin, A. W. (1999). Student involvement: A developmental theory for higher education. *Journal of College Student Development, 40*(5), 518-529.

Colvin, J. W., & Ashman, M. (2010). Roles, risks, and benefits of peer mentoring relationships in higher education. *Mentoring & Tutoring: Partnership in Learning, 18*(2), 121-134.

Cuseo, J. (2007). Seven central principles of student success: Key processes associated with positive student outcomes. *E-Source for College Transitions, 4*(6), 3-5. https://sc.edu/nrc/system/pub_files/ES_4-6_Jul07.pdf

Dias, D. (2022) The higher education commitment challenge: Impacts of physical and cultural dimensions in the first-year students' sense of belonging. *Education Sciences, 12*(4), 231. https://doi.org/10.3390/educsci12040231

Duerr, J. L. T. (2020). *Connecting to campus from afar: How commuter students cultivate their sense of belonging through technology* (Publication No. 27743802) [Doctoral dissertation, California State University, Fresno]. ProQuest Dissertations Publishing.

Dungy, G., & Peck, A. (2019). How campus activities can lead the modern university: Five imperatives. *Journal of Campus Activities Practice and Scholarship 1*(1), 6-13. https://doi.org/10.52499/2019002

Ellison, B., & Braxton, J. M. (2022). Reviewing, theorizing, and looking ahead. The relationship between college students' sense of belonging and persistence. In E. M. Bentrim & G. W. Henning (Eds.), *The impact of a sense of belonging in college* (pp. 3-20). Stylus.

Gopalan, M., & Brady, S. T. (2020). College students' sense of belonging: A national perspective. *Educational Researcher, 49*(2), 134-137. https://doi.org/10.3102/0013189X19897622

Handy, R. C. (2017). *The relationship between leadership skills and academic performance among dyslexic students.* [Doctoral dissertation, Our Lady of the Lake University]. ProQuest Dissertations Publishing.

Komives, S. R. (2019). Engagement with campus activities matters: Toward a new era of educationally purposeful activities. *Journal of Campus Activities Practice and Scholarship, 1*(1), 14-25. https://doi.org/10.52499/2019003

Kouzoukas, G. (2020). Engaging first-generation students. In S. J. Quaye, S. R. Harper, & S. L. Pendakur (Eds.), *Student engagement in higher education: Theoretical perspectives and practical approaches for diverse populations* (pp. 287-306). Routledge.

Kuh, G. D., Kinzie, J., Schuh, J. H., Whitt, E. J., & Associates. (2005). *Student success in college: Creating conditions that matter.* Jossey-Bass.

Lave, J., & Wenger, E. (1991). *Situated learning: Legitimate peripheral participation.* Cambridge University Press. https://psycnet.apa.org/doi/10.1017/CBO9780511815355

Loper, K. R. (2022). University belonging scale: Defining and evaluating students' sense of belonging to their university. [Doctoral dissertation, Oklahoma State University, Stillwater]. https://shareok.org/bitstream/handle/11244/337173/Loper_okstate_0664D_17675.pdf?sequence=1&isAllowed=y

Museus, S. D., Griffin, K. A., & Quaye, S. J. (2020). Engaging students of color. In S. J. Quaye, S. R. Harper, & S. L. Pendakur (Eds.), *Student engagement in higher education: Theoretical perspectives and practical approaches for diverse populations* (pp. 17-35). Routledge.

National Association for Campus Activities. (2023a). Defining terms. https://www.naca.org/resources/professional-development/defining-terms.html

National Association for Campus Activities. (2023b). NACA competencies for student leaders. https://www.naca.org/resource/competencies-for-student-leaders-2022-pdf.html

National Association for Campus Activities. (2023c). Employability skills assessment. https://www.naca.org/resources/employability-skills-assessment.html

Nunn, L. M. (2021). *College belonging: How first-year and first-generation students navigate campus life.* Rutgers University Press.

Peck, A., McCullar, S., Rosch, D. M., DeSawal, D., & Russell Krebs, S. (2020). Lessons from a pandemic: The value of campus activities professionals. *Journal of Campus Activities Practice and Scholarship, 2*(2), 5-12. https://doi.org/10.52499/2020008

Stadler, M. J., Becker, N., Grieff, S., & Spinath, F. M. (2015). The complex route to success: Complex problem-solving skills in the prediction of university success. *Higher Education Research & Development, 35*(2), 365-379. https://doi.org/10.1080/07294360.2015.1087387

Strayhorn, T. L. (2019). *College students' sense of belonging: A key to educational success for all students* (2nd ed.). Routledge.

Strayhorn, T. L. (2022). Rearticulating "cultural navigators": An equity-minded framework for student success. *New Directions for Higher Education, 2022*(197), 23-34. https://doi.org/10.1002/he.20424

Teaching & Learning Resources Center (n.d.) *High-impact practices: Enhancing the student experience.* The Ohio State University. https://teaching.resources.osu.edu/teaching-topics/high-impact-practices-enhancing

Tinto, V. (1987, November 20). *The principles of effective retention* (ED301267). ERIC. https://eric.ed.gov/?id=ED301267

Tinto, V. (1997). Classrooms as communities: Exploring the educational character of student persistence. *Journal of Higher Education, 68*(6), 599-623. https://doi.org/10.1080/00221546.1997.11779003

Vaccaro, A., & Newman, B. (2022). Theoretical foundations for sense of belonging in college. In E. M. Bentrim & G. W. Henning (Eds.), *The impact of a sense of belonging in college* (pp. 3-20). Stylus.

van der Meer, J., Skalicky, J., Speed, H., & Young, D. G. (2022). Focusing on the development of the whole student: An international comparative study of the perceived benefits of peer leadership in higher education. *Open Journal of Social Sciences, 10*(3), 14-35. https://doi.org/10.4236/jss.2022.103002

Part 3

**Conclusion:
Tying it all Together**

Chapter 9

Conclusion: Charting a Path Forward

Bryce D. Bunting
Brigham Young University

Dallin George Young
University of Georgia

We began this report by echoing the claim that "interactions with peers [are] probably the most pervasive and powerful force in student persistence and degree completion (Pascarella & Terenzini, 2005, p. 615). As we conclude, we want to emphasize that this "powerful force" does not simply benefit the *recipients* of peer leadership. As is apparent from the results of the ISPL-US, peer leadership can make a powerful contribution to the retention, persistence, completion, and belonging of those who *serve as peer leaders* (PLs).

We call upon higher education leaders to adopt a reconceptualized view of the purposes of peer leadership. Specifically, organized, institutionally sanctioned peer leadership programs need to be viewed as more than a remedial tactic or strategy deployed to rescue students on the margins. Instead, *being* a PL is an intervention in and of itself. As the authors of this report have collectively argued, providing peer leadership opportunities to all students—particularly those from historically underserved and excluded populations—is a powerful way for institutions to, in the words of Lisa Nunn (2021), *offer belonging* to their students.

As a reminder the specific research questions that guided our analysis were

- Can peer leadership be considered a high-impact practice (HIP)? What evidence does the ISPL-US provide to justify this claim? And how can the PL experience be further refined and improved to better align with the characteristics of HIPs?

- Who has access to peer leadership experiences? What do the results of the ISPL-US reveal about the experiences of PLs from minoritized populations?

- What are the key issues, emerging trends, and potential avenues for future research that are illuminated by the results of the 2023 ISPL-US study?

We hope that readers have discovered insights and understanding relative to these questions throughout their reading of this report. Nonetheless, we conclude the report with a summary of how the 2023 ISPL-US helps to answer these questions. Additionally, we invite readers to consider the implications and application of these ideas for their own practice, or their own scholarly inquiries related to peer leadership.

Peer Leadership as a High-Impact Practice

The findings of the ISPL-US provide growing support for the claim that, when well-designed and administered, peer leadership aligns with the definition of HIPs put forward by Kuh (2008) in his foundational work on HIPs. Indeed, peer leadership is (a) widely implemented; (b) associated with high levels of student engagement, deep and integrated learning, and general academic gains for all students; and (c) particularly impactful for historically underserved and excluded students (Finley & McNair, 2013; NSSE, 2021; Zilvinskis et al., 2022). Additionally, our analysis of the ISPL-US data provided robust evidence that peer leadership meets a number of the characteristics of HIPs identified by Kuh & O'Donnell (2013), including

- significant investment of time and effort by students over an extended period of time,
- interactions with faculty and peers about substantive matters,
- experiences with diversity, wherein students are exposed to and must contend with people and circumstances that differ from those with which students are familiar,
- frequent, timely, and constructive feedback, and
- periodic, structured opportunities to reflect and integrate learning.

We were encouraged by the fact that, in general, ISPL-US respondents described that their PL experiences met these criteria and that they were satisfied with their experience. However, there were some notable gaps in their experiences related to these defining characteristics of HIPs.

First, while participants reported that their PL experiences provided meaningful opportunities to interact with faculty, there is room for improvement. Just over half of the respondents (56%) reported that their PL experiences "increased" or "greatly increased" their meaningful interactions with faculty. In contrast, 64.8% of respondents reported that these same experiences "increased" or "greatly increased" their meaningful interactions with staff. Thus, at least for the participants in this study, peer leadership is still a staff-run experience. To be clear, these interactions with staff members are important and provide PLs with valuable support and supervision in their work. However, there is strong evidence of the unique power in providing students with opportunities to develop relationships with and be mentored by faculty members (e.g., Felten et al., 2016; Mayhew et al., 2016; Schreiner et al., 2020). Consequently, we encourage practitioners to continue to find ways to integrate faculty members into the PL experience. This could include embedding PLs in first-year and gateway courses taught by faculty members, appointing qualified faculty members to direct and administer PL initiatives, involving faculty members in training PLs, or any other activities that bring PLs and faculty members into sustained relationship with each other. This focus on PL–faculty interactions is one way of structuring the PL experience to facilitate *legitimate peripheral participation* (Lave & Wenger, 1991) for PLs that allows them to not only get to know faculty members, but to step into a role as co-participants with faculty in the work of supporting student learning.

Second, our findings raise questions about the degree to which PLs view their experiences as rigorous or as deep learning experiences. While the ISPL-US certainly provided evidence that some PLs were experiencing learning and growth in their role within particular domains (e.g., experiences with students from backgrounds different than PLs' own, time management, interpersonal communication skills, leadership), their reported growth was not universally high across all domains. For example, 30% of the respondents from the overall sample reported that their PL experience(s) had no impact on their academic skills and 24.4% of respondents indicated that being a PL had no impact on their desire to keep learning after graduation. Similarly, 23.6% of respondents indicated that their written communication skills were not influenced by their PL experiences and 26% reported that their ability to share ideas with others in writing had not been influenced.

In general, PLs view their growth as being limited to social or interpersonal domains (e.g., interpersonal communication skills, leadership, teamwork, collaboration). While they do develop academic skills, the ISPL-US data illuminate a noteworthy gap between reported academic outcomes and social and interpersonal outcomes. Additionally, 26% of participants reported that serving as a PL had no impact on their ability to succeed in a full-time job after graduation. This was surprising given that these same respondents reported significant growth in time and project management skills, creativity, problem-solving and critical thinking—all abilities that matter in employment settings. While PLs seem to be learning in their role, they may not recognize how beneficial this learning will be in the future.

Consequently, there are opportunities to both raise expectations related to what PLs will learn in their role, and then communicate these high expectations to PLs. This has implications from marketing and recruitment, to training, to the supervision and mentoring provided by faculty and staff, and maybe most importantly the support provided to PLs as they transition out of their leadership roles. Those who support PLs should look for opportunities to engage them in frequent reflection on how their experiences are positioning them for improved academic success and future employability. In sum, we assert that PLs are experiencing academic and career-related growth—they may just not recognize this growth without being invited to reflect on and articulate this learning and how it can be applied to both their current and future experiences. By reflecting on and articulating how their PL experiences are preparing them for future roles, PLs are much more likely to see their leadership experiences as legitimate or authentic practices that hold value in real-world contexts outside and beyond the college experience.

Finally, the ISPL-US data point to the fact that peer leadership could be a more writing-intensive experience. As discussed, one fourth of the participants in the study reported that their PL experiences had no impact on their writing abilities. Further, we found it disheartening that fewer than half of the PLs in the sample (45.4%) reported engaging in regular written reflections, and that a meager 8.7% reported that they had been invited to create a portfolio documenting their learning in their role. We invite those who administer PL programs to evaluate the role that writing currently plays in the PL experiences on their campus and to identify ways in which writing might become a more prominent aspect of these experiences. Just as PLs may be developing more significant academic and employability skills than they realize, we suspect the same may be true with their writing abilities. Those who support and supervise PLs have an opportunity to help them see that the PL-related writing they are doing—incident reports in residence life, program summaries, tutoring notes, and the like—are, again, legitimate and authentic forms of written communication that offer experience in the kinds of writing that they will encounter once they leave college.

Peer Leadership as Legitimate Peripheral Participation: The Experiences of Peer Leaders on the Margins

It is important that we acknowledge that our sample is not representative of higher education broadly. It is strongly overrepresented by four-year institutions, which are more frequently White in areas that are overrepresented by White people compared to national demographics. Consequently, care should be taken to avoid overgeneralizing participation patterns in peer leadership evident in our sample to the broader population of PLs in the United States. Nonetheless, we find it helpful to point out that Black, Latino/a, first-generation, and Pell-eligible students were all significantly underrepresented among those participants who reported having served as PLs.

At least among our participants, it appears that students from marginalized sub-populations are not participating in peer leadership at the same rate as their White, middle-class, and continuing generation peers. This is not likely due to any functional barriers to access because nominal access to peer leadership experiences would be open to all students on all campuses. Instead, we suspect that this is an issue of *practical access*, in that particular students are not choosing to participate, or feel that they cannot participate, because of structural aspects of the experience, including the way these positions are marketed, who they are marketed to, the time that is required, or the compensation (or lack thereof) that is offered. We recommend that institutions carefully audit the peer leadership experiences offered on their campus to identify hidden barriers that may be preventing some students from participating.

However, for the students from these underrepresented groups who reported having served as a PL, the experience had an outsized positive impact on their sense of belonging when compared to their peers. Seen through the theoretical lens provided by Lave and Wenger (1991), being a PL seemed to provide opportunities for marginalized students to experience a stronger sense of belonging by engaging in *legitimate peripheral participation.* Peer leadership offered access to the relationships, authentic activities, and learning that, together, signaled to PLs with marginalized identities that they were contributing and valued members of the campus community. This was true for all three of the domains of belonging identified by Nunn (2021): (a) social, (b) academic, and (c) campus-community belonging. First, participants who identified as first-generation, Pell-eligible, or Students of Color (except students who identified as Native Hawaiian or Pacific Islander) were more likely to report that their meaningful social interactions with peers had increased as a direct result of their peer leadership experiences (see Table 2.7).

Second, ISPL-US participants with minoritized identities were more likely than their peers to have reported that various aspects of their academic belonging had increased as a direct result of their experiences as a PL (see Table 2.10). First-generation students who reported serving as PLs were more likely to report that their PL experiences had led to gains in academic skills, GPA, and overall academic performance than their continuing generation peers. Similarly, PLs from low-income backgrounds were more likely to report that serving as a PL had led to gains in both academic skill and overall academic performance (but not GPA) than their non-Pell-eligible peers. While this trend of increased sense of academic belonging was not as strong when comparing White and non-White students, it was still present. In comparison to participants who identified as White, participants who identified as students of color were more likely to report that their experiences as a PL had led to increased GPA and increases in overall academic performance (again, except for students who identified as Native Hawaiian or Pacific Islander).

Finally, for PLs in the sample who reported marginalized identities, serving as a PL seemed to have a particularly strong impact on their overall sense of *campus-community belonging* (see Table 2.12). For both first-generation and Pell-eligible PLs in the study, they were more likely to report that their experiences had directly led to increases in (a) their feelings of belonging at their institution, (b) their desire to stay and graduate at their institution, and (c) their feelings of contribution to their campus community. As for both social and academic belonging, the direct impact of peer leadership in campus-community belonging was more mixed across racial and ethnic groups.

More research should be conducted to examine why the experiences of PLs who identify as Native Hawaiian and Pacific Islander are different. However, we want to note that across all participants in the ISPL-US study, less than 1% identified as Native Hawaiian or Pacific Islander, so we suspect that some of these differences may be an artifact of exceedingly small sample sizes.

Key Issues and Trends Illuminated by the 2023 ISPL-US

The results of the ISPL-US provide important insight into several emerging issues, including the role of PL compensation and its implication for access and inclusion, the impact of PL experiences on the development of employability outcomes, and the way that peer leadership can contribute to belonging among those who serve as PLs.

Compensation

As discussed in Chapter 5, the results of our study point to a troubling relationship between peer leadership experiences and the *working student dilemma* (Burnside et al., 2019). Over one third of our respondents indicated that they received no compensation for their work. Uncompensated peer leadership work was particularly notable among socially oriented PL roles (e.g., campus activities and orientation leaders), with just over 50% of the respondents in these roles indicating that they worked on a voluntary basis. We also want to note that this same group of PLs in socially oriented roles were far more likely to identify as Black or Latino/a. Thus, there seem to be potential equity issues at work here. Additionally, just under one third of our participants reported that they were eligible for Pell Grant funding. Finally, as discussed previously our analysis also suggests that, for most PLs, their work requires a significant investment of time and energy; over 80% of our participants reported that, on average, they spend six or more hours per week performing their PL responsibilities.

Together, this constellation of data points raises critical questions about who is and is not compensated for their PL work and who legitimately has the time to devote to uncompensated PL roles. Quite simply, we are concerned with the distinct possibility that there are many students enrolled at U.S. institutions who are qualified to serve as PLs and who would be interested in these roles, but who cannot afford to invest the time required without receiving some sort of meaningful compensation. Again, we point to the work of Ardoin and martinez (2019) and their observation that "to be a student leader, one must have a degree of freedom, whether that is financial or time" (p. 41).

While institutions often market PL experiences as a resume builder—and our data provide convincing evidence that it indeed can be—past research has suggested that voluntary PL roles are not associated with any statistically significant gains in skill development, institutional interaction, academic commitment, or employability outcomes (Young & Keup, 2018). Consequently, we suggest that institutions who engage PLs in uncompensated and time-intensive roles may at times be guilty of an inadvertent "bait and switch" by recruiting students with the promise of a growth-promoting volunteer experience that may not be as impactful as advertised. Ultimately, if PLs are doing the work of the institution, they should be compensated accordingly.

As we conclude our discussion of compensation for peer leadership, we offer a strong caution to institutions who rely heavily on volunteer PLs. Without careful attention on the part of institutional leaders, voluntary peer leadership can:

- be exploitative,
- be a barrier to access and inclusion,
- be a subtle signal of low expectations for the importance of the PL role on campus, and
- significantly limit the learning and growth experienced by PLs in their role.

We recommend that institutional leaders and program administrators make a commitment to evaluating compensation structures for PLs on their campus to ensure that the pitfalls listed above are avoided. A failure to do so may negate the high-impact potential of peer leadership and, ironically, become a barrier to PLs' success and thriving.

Employability Outcomes

While the PLs in our study reported significant gains across many skills and abilities, fewer than half (47.4%) reported that their ability to succeed in full-time employment after graduation had increased as a direct result of their PL experiences. Initially, these two findings seemed to us to be at odds. However, as we continued to wrestle with this seeming contradiction, we arrived at the hypothesis that many of the participants in ISPL-US did not fully recognize that what they were learning from their experiences would benefit them in their future careers.

To help PLs better recognize, articulate, and appreciate how their work is preparing them for post-college employment, we recommend, first, that institutions work to partner with their career services and career advisement units to ensure that the PL experiences being offered do indeed offer meaningful opportunities to develop key outcomes valued by employers. These outcomes can then be clearly highlighted in marketing and recruitment materials and prioritized in the assessment plans that are developed to evaluate the PL experience. Additionally, those who supervise and mentor PLs should look for ways to have more frequent reflective conversations with PLs about what they are learning, how this learning connects to future roles, and what additional learning PLs could pursue to align with their future goals. This reflection-in-practice can provide authentic opportunities for PLs to recognize how they are participating in and contributing to a community of practice and becoming a skilled and experienced member of that community. This would naturally lead to opportunities to engage PLs in writing-intensive practices such as clearly and concisely representing their learning on a resume.

We also encourage campus leaders to explore how e-portfolios could be used to support PLs in reflecting on and providing evidence of their achievement of employability-related outcomes. The NACA Student

Leadership Competencies and NACA Employability Skills Assessment described by Sarah Keeling in Chapter 8 could provide helpful guidance. Similarly, campuses might consider including peer leadership experiences on co-curricular transcripts.

Sense of Belonging

Participants in the ISPL-US reported high levels of sense of belonging, particularly those PLs from historically marginalized demographic groups. But to return to one of the themes we introduced in Chapter 1, experiencing belonging in the PL role is not a foregone conclusion; the degree to which peer leadership contributes to belonging is dependent on the quality or anatomy of the experience.

Working to design peer leadership experience as a pathway to belonging seems especially important considering the ISPL-US data on what motivated participants to seek out PL roles. Readers may recall from Chapter 2 that first-generation and Pell-eligible students were significantly more likely to have reported that they were motivated to become a PL in order to be more involved in and develop relationships within their university community (see Tables 2.4 and 2.5). Based on these data, there is evidence that students from underrepresented groups often view becoming a PL as a viable route to gaining belonging and membership. Consequently, those who design and administer these programs have a responsibility to deliver on the promise of peer leadership as a pathway toward belonging.

The *modes of transition* discussed previously (*community, participation, and becoming;* Young and Bunting, 2024) offer a helpful framework for considering both why and how serving as a PL can contribute to a sense of belonging for students. First, when peer leadership offers regular opportunities to interact with peers, staff, and faculty (e.g., regular classroom interactions, training meetings and workshops, ongoing mentoring and supervision from faculty and staff) in service of a common goal or purpose, PLs experience powerful forms of *community*. These community features, including opportunities to reflect, engage with diverse others, receive feedback, and share one's learning in public ways, align with the characteristics of HIPs and provide a rich learning environment where PLs experience both the challenge and support (Sanford, 1967) needed to succeed and thrive.

Second, when institutions view peer leadership as an opportunity for students to *participate* as legitimate members of the campus community alongside faculty, advisors, and student affairs professionals in the central work of supporting learning, they are positioned to experience a sense of belonging distinct from what comes through their friendships and social interactions. Working as a member of an institutional team toward a shared purpose or goal communicates to PLs that they are competent, valued, and play an essential role on campus. For a student who may have entered college experiencing some degree of *belonging uncertainty* (Walton & Cohen, 2007), being invited to participate in meaningful work in these ways provides an important signal of membership and belonging.

Finally, moving into any new PL role, whether as an orientation leader, Supplemental Instruction leader, campus activities leader, peer advisor, or any other form of peer leadership, involves students in reshaping and refining their identities. Put another way, being a PL is a process of *becoming*. Indeed, as PLs strengthen their academic and interpersonal skills, they experience individual identity development and *become* more experienced learners and leaders. But this becoming is not limited to individual development. PLs also experience shifts in their group identities as they *become* members of a new community made up of the peers they support, the other PLs in their program, and the faculty and staff with whom they interact. Thus, becoming a peer mentor, like all learning experiences, is an experience of identity; it has the potential to transform student identities at both an individual and a community level.

This focus on and prioritization of providing experiences that facilitate *becoming* has important implications for fostering all three of the domains of belonging outlined by Nunn (2021). First, as PLs carry out their responsibilities, they have opportunities to become more academically competent and confident, which deepens their sense of *academic belonging*. Through their interactions with their peers, they develop a stronger degree of *social belonging*. Finally, as PLs participate alongside faculty, staff, and other institutional leaders in the core work of education, they *become* members of the broader campus community and experience *campus-community belonging*. Thus, in attending to *becoming* at both an individual and a community level, institutions can offer a powerful pathway toward belonging for students who serve as PLs.

Recommendations for Future Research

Throughout the report, our colleagues have provided thoughtful analysis of the results of the ISPL-US along with insight into what these findings mean for practice on our campuses. As we looked across the chapters, we identified three thematic areas where consensus coalesced in identifying promising paths of future inquiry: (a) forms of participation; (b) the trajectory of participation in PL experiences; and (c) equity, belonging, and mental health.

The findings in each chapter in the report pointed to the importance of PLs' relationships with those who supervise and train them. These relationships were named, either directly or indirectly, to provide crucial clues into the PL experience. In this vein was a uniform call for what Lave and Wenger (1991) have described as *legitimate peripheral participation* in the activities of the functional area where the PL is working. The field needs more research aimed at understanding the conditions under which this kind of participation is happening. This line of inquiry has become even more important with the increase in PLs who primarily work in online or virtual settings, where there is potential for peer leadership to become merely transactional. Research should be done to determine how these PL opportunities can be structured to provide students with a high-impact and authentic participatory experience.

Additionally, findings pointed to a need for a deeper understanding of the overall *trajectory of participation* (Lave & Wenger, 1991) in PL experiences. Findings showed that students have complex sets of motivators for engaging in PL roles, including desires to contribute to the educational activities of the institution, to develop their own human capital, and to earn money. The reasons motivating engagement in PL roles have an important influence on the overall trajectory of participation and the learning that can occur in these experiences. Prior research has consistently established the relationship between the time a student spends in a PL role and increased outcomes (e.g., Roscoe & Chi, 2007; Topping, 2005; Young & Keup, 2018; Young et al., 2023). This raises questions about the temporal aspects of the trajectory of participation. How does motivation set the stage for the forms of participation that students expect? What kinds of PL experiences are appropriate for students to engage in early in their educational careers, such as their first or second year? How much time in the PL role is necessary to experience deep and transformative learning? And, is there a point of diminishing returns? If authentic participation matters, then how do time in the role and the variety of roles interact? Finally, there are questions about the long-term impacts of participation in PL experiences. What are the durable benefits of participation several years down the road? How do graduates make meaning of participation and their own trajectories five, 10, or 15 years down the road?

Finally, we were struck by the thoughtful discourse throughout the report that connected issues of equity, belonging, and mental health. For example, in Chapter 4, Tori Negash discussed the fact that the complex nature of PL roles can lead to stress, burnout, and secondary trauma. Yet, the sense of belonging offered by the PL role can serve as a protective factor and mitigate the impact of stress on mental health, especially for students from minoritized and marginalized backgrounds. This opens an important set of practical and ethical questions for those who plan to engage with PLs. First, how does the PL experience impact students' mental health? Are burnout, stress, or anxiety more or less prevalent among students serving in PL roles? In what ways are institutional actors exploiting PLs and how is that contributing to stress and burnout, particularly when PLs' work is not structured in ways that foster belonging or that offers no financial compensation? What are the equity implications for students who perceive the stress and potential exploitation of PLs and who decide not to participate as a form of self-protection, despite the potential benefits?

We invite scholar-practitioners to join us in pursuing deeper and more meaningful research on PL experiences than we have explored to this point. This will help us refine the theory-practice of peer leadership, as well as the lived experiences of students who participate in these roles. A commitment to exploring these and related research questions will better position the field to offer PL experiences that deliver on the promise of transformation and becoming, while minimizing the potential for exclusion and exploitation.

References

Ardoin, S. (2020). Engaging poor and working-class students. In S. J. Quaye, S. R. Harper, & S. L. Pendakur (Eds.), *Student engagement in higher education: Theoretical perspectives and practical approaches for diverse populations* (pp. 307-323). Routledge.

Barnett, R. (2009). Knowing and becoming in the higher education curriculum. *Studies in Higher Education, 34*(4), 429-440. https://doi.org/10.1080/03075070902771978

Burnside, O., Wesley, A., Wesaw, A., & Parnell, A. (2019). Employing student success: A comprehensive examination of on-campus student employment. *NASPA-Student Affairs Administrators in Higher Education.*

Felten, P., Gardner, J. N., Schroeder, C. C., Lambert, L. M., Barefoot, B. O., & Hrabowski, F. A. (2016). *The undergraduate experience: Focusing institutions on what matters most.* John Wiley & Sons.

Finley, A., & McNair, T. (2013). Assessing underserved students' engagement in high impact practices. Association of American Colleges & Universities. https://www.aacu.org/assessinghips/report

Kuh, G. D., & O'Donnell, K. (2013). Ensuring quality and taking high-impact practices to scale. *Peer Review, 15*(2), 32-33. https://link.gale.com/apps/doc/A339018909/AONE?u=byuprovo&sid=googleScholar&xid=39de3a32

Lave, J., & Wenger, E. (1991). *Situated learning: Legitimate peripheral participation.* Cambridge University Press.

Mayhew, M. J., Rockenbach, A. N., Bowman, N. A., Seifert, T. A., & Wolniak, G. C. (2016). *How college affects students: 21st century evidence that higher education works* (Vol. 1). John Wiley & Sons.

National Survey of Student Engagement. (2021). *Engagement insights: Survey findings on the quality of undergraduate education.* Indiana University Center for Postsecondary Research.

Nunn, L. M. (2021). *College belonging: How first-year and first-generation students navigate campus life.* Rutgers University Press.

Pascarella, E. T., & Terenzini, P. T. (2005). *How college affects students: A third decade of research* (Vol. 2). Jossey-Bass.

Roscoe, R. D., & Chi, M. T. (2007). Understanding tutor learning: Knowledge-building and knowledge-telling in peer tutors' explanations and questions. *Review of Educational Research, 77*(4), 534-574. https://doi.org/10.3102/0034654307309920

Sanford, N. (1967). *Where colleges fail: A study of the student as a person.* Jossey Bass.

Schreiner, L. A., Louis, M. C., & Nelson, D. D. (Eds.). (2020). *Thriving in transitions: A research-based approach to college student success.* University of South Carolina, National Resource Center for The First-Year Experience and Students in Transition.

Topping, K. J. (2005). Trends in peer learning. *Educational Psychology, 25*(6), 631-645. https://doi.org/10.1080/01443410500345172

Walton, G. M., & Cohen, G. L. (2007). A question of belonging: Race, social fit, and achievement. *Journal of Personality and Social Psychology, 92*(1), 82-96. https://doi.org/10.1037/0022-3514.92.1.82

Young, D. G., & Bunting, B. D. (2024). *Rethinking student transitions: How community, participation, and becoming can help higher education deliver on its promise.* University of South Carolina, National Resource Center for The First-Year Experience and Students in Transition.

Young, D. G. & Keup, J. R. (2018). To pay or not to pay: The influence of compensation as an external reward on learning outcomes of peer leaders. *Journal of College Student Development, 59*(2), 159-176. https://doi.org/10.1353/csd.2018.0015

Young, D. G., Zeng, W., Skalicky, J., & van der Meer, J. (2023). The quality and quantity of participation in peer leader experiences and student outcomes: A cross-national validation of constructs and predictive model. *Research in Higher Education,* 1-21. https://doi.org/10.1007/s11162-023-09765-4

Zilvinskis, J., Kinzie, J., Daday, J., O'Donnell, K., & Vande Zande, C. (2022). When done well: 14 years of chasing an admonition. In J. Zilvinskis, Kinzie, J., Daday, K. O'Donnell, & C. Vande Zande (Eds.), *Delivering on the promise of high-impact practices: Research and models for achieving equity, fidelity, impact, and scale* (pp. 1–10). Routledge.

Appendix A

International Survey of Peer Leaders - US 2022-23 Administration Survey Methods

Project Background

The International Survey of Peer Leaders is a project that grew out of the success of the 2013 administration of the U.S.-based National Survey of Peer Leaders created and carried out by the research team at the National Resource Center for The First-Year Experience and Students in Transition. This led to the development of the first administration of the International Survey of Peer leaders when representatives from Australia, Canada, New Zealand, South Africa, and the United Kingdom were involved in the development of an International Survey of Peer Leaders that was conducted in five English-speaking countries across the globe between August 2014 and January 2016.

Questionnaire Construction

The 2022-24 International Survey of Peer Leaders represents an update to the previous administration and was designed to allow the researchers involved in this project to pursue answers to the following overarching research questions:

1. What are the roles in which student peer leaders are engaged?

2. What are the structural characteristics of peer leader experiences?

3. What is the relationship between the characteristics of peer leader experiences and reported outcomes?

The international approach to the research held as guiding principles that the questionnaires for each participating country should strike a balance between consistency to facilitate cross-national comparisons while allowing customization for each participating region to be able to respond to its unique cultural approach to higher education and to answer compelling research questions germane to that locality.

The US-based version of the ISPL (ISPL-US) questionnaire was developed by representatives of the National Resource Center by reviewing the base international version of the questionnaire and revising wording and adding questions as deemed important to answering questions for the US context. Notably, the US team created and included additional questions aimed at providing insight into how the peer-leader experience in the US represents a high-impact practice following the elements listed by Kuh and O'Donnell (2013). The ISPL-US questionnaire can be found in Appendix B.

Recruitment and Sample

Recruitment of the sample of participants for the ISPL-US occurred at three levels. First, the country project coordinator reached out to prominent higher education professional organizations that represented functional areas where students in peer leader roles were used extensively. These professional organizations agreed to help recruit campus contacts who would administer the ISPL-US at their respective institutions. The professional organizations who partnered in the administration of the survey included the International Center for Supplemental Instruction, the National Association for Campus Activities, NACADA – The Global Community for Academic Advising, and NODA – the Association for Orientation, Transition, and Retention in Higher Education as well as the National Resource Center for The First-Year Experience and Students in Transition.

The second level of recruitment of participants occurred at the institution level. Organizational partners forwarded a recruitment message to potential campus contacts through various communication channels including listservs, newsletters, and social media channels. Campus project coordinators who agreed to participate agreed to assist in the recruitment of students on their campuses by identifying the various places where peer leaders were used on campus to capture a sample of students who are representative of the peer leader roles at the participating institution. A total of 27 institutions participated in the survey.

At the third level, campus project coordinators forwarded recruitment messages to students at their institutions inviting them to participate in an online survey. Campus project coordinators were given instructions to forward an initial invitation and at least one follow-up reminder across one month. Given the staggered timing of the administration, institutions could have participated at any time between October 1, 2022, and March 30, 2023, when the administration window was closed. This resulted in 1,533 responses from students, of which 1,399 reported currently or ever having served in a PL role on campus.

Analyses

The sample data's analyses were conducted at the descriptive level. Comprehensive frequency distribution and sample percentages for each item reported throughout the research report were tabulated for the sample in total across peer leader role. Frequencies and percentages for the overall sample are presented in Appendix C.

Appendix B

International Survey of Peer Leaders Student Questionnaire - United States

Instructions for Participants

The purpose of this international survey is to gather information about your experience as a peer leader. We define a peer leader as *an **undergraduate or postgraduate student** who has been selected to serve as a mentor, educator, or advisor to other students through a position with a campus-run organization.*

As you answer each question, please reflect on your experience(s) as a peer leader. Your responses will be used to help researchers study and better understand the peer leadership experience. Your participation in the survey is anonymous as we do not ask for personal information that can identify you. In addition, all individual responses will be kept confidential and only the pooled data of many participants will be reported. Responding to this survey will take approximately 10-15 minutes.

Note, this is the second administration of the International Survey of Peer Leaders and it is possible you participated in the first administration several years ago. If this is the case, we ask that you respond to questions in a way that reflects your current views about the peer leader roles that you engage in at present or have undertaken in the past.

Before we begin asking you about your peer leader experiences, we would like to learn a little bit about your background and who you are:

College/Universty Study Details

Q1. What college or university do you attend?____

Q2. What is your class standing (based on number of full-time equivalent years attended at any university or college)?

- ❏ First-year student
- ❏ Second-year student
- ❏ Third-year student
- ❏ Fourth-year student
- ❏ Fifth-year student
- ❏ Nondegree-seeking student
- ❏ Other (please specify):____

Q3. What is the broad subject area of your major? If you have more than one major, please select all subject areas that apply. If you have not officially declared a major, please answer undeclared.

- ❒ Agriculture
- ❒ Architecture and related services
- ❒ Visual and performing arts
- ❒ Business, management, marketing, and related support services
- ❒ Communications
- ❒ Education
- ❒ Engineering and computer science
- ❒ Health professions and related programs
- ❒ Human and consumer sciences
- ❒ Humanities (e.g., English, History, Languages, etc.)
- ❒ Legal professions and studies
- ❒ Library science
- ❒ Life sciences (e.g., Biology, Botany, Genetics, etc.)
- ❒ Mathematics, statistics, and analytics
- ❒ Natural resources and conservation
- ❒ Parks, recreation, leisure, and fitness studies
- ❒ Physical sciences (e.g., Chemistry, Physics, Astronomy, etc.)
- ❒ Public administration and social service
- ❒ Social sciences (e.g., Anthropology, Political Science, Psychology, etc.)
- ❒ Theology and religious vocations
- ❒ Vocational and technical fields
- ❒ Other (please specify):____
  Undeclared

Q4. What was your cumulative GPA at the start of the current term?_______________________

Q5. During the school year, which of the following best describes your housing?
- ❒ On-campus housing
- ❒ Off-campus housing, sponsored by your college or university
- ❒ Off campus housing, not sponsored by your college or university

Q6. Have any of your parents or guardians earned a four-year college degree?
- ❒ Yes
- ❒ No
- ❒ I don't know

Q7. Are you eligible for financial aid under the Pell Grant program?

- ❏ Yes
- ❏ No
- ❏ I don't know

Demographic Details

Q8. What is your age?

- ❏ Younger than 18
- ❏ 18-20
- ❏ 21-25
- ❏ 26-30
- ❏ 31-35
- ❏ Older than 35

Q9. What is your gender?

- ❏ Agender
- ❏ Man
- ❏ Woman
- ❏ Nonbinary/Genderqueer/Genderfluid
- ❏ Two spirit
- ❏ Another identity not listed here (please specify):_______________________________________
- ❏ Prefer not to say

Q10. What is your residency status?

- ❏ In-state student
- ❏ Out-of-state student
- ❏ International student

Q11. What is your race or ethnicity? (Select all that apply.)

- ❏ American Indian or Alaska Native
- ❏ Asian or Asian American
- ❏ Black or African American
- ❏ Hispanic, Chicano/a, or Latino/a
- ❏ Native Hawaiian or other Pacific Islander
- ❏ White
- ❏ Other
- ❏ I prefer not to respond to this question.

Q12. Using the slider below, please rate your agreement to the following:

	Strongly Disagree	Strongly Agree
I am a member of a racial or ethnic group that has historically been oppressed in my current country of residence.		

Peer Leader Experiences (Including paid and volunteer roles)

We define a peer leader as an undergraduate (or postgraduate) student who has been selected to serve as a mentor, educator, or advisor to other students through a position with a campus-run organization.

Q13. Are you currently serving as a peer leader?

- ☐ Yes *(Go To Q15)*
- ☐ No *(Go To Q14)*
- ☐ I don't know *(Go To Q14)*

Q14. Have you ever served as a peer leader?

- ☐ Yes *(Go To Q15)*
- ☐ No *(Go To End)*
- ☐ I don't know *(Go To End)*

Type of Peer Leader Experience(s)

Q15. What type of campus-based organization have you worked for as a peer leader, either currently or in the past? (Select all that apply.)

- ☐ Athletics
- ☐ Academic – peer advisor
- ☐ Academic – Supplemental Instruction leader
- ☐ Academic – tutor
- ☐ Academic – other (e.g., teaching assistant, lab assistant) (Please specify)
- ☐ Admissions
- ☐ Campus activities
- ☐ Community service or service-learning
- ☐ Counseling or mental health
- ☐ Financial literacy
- ☐ First-year experience
- ☐ Greek life (i.e., social fraternity or sorority)
- ☐ International student office
- ☐ Judicial affairs or student conduct
- ☐ Multicultural affairs
- ☐ Orientation (e.g., new student, extended, or summer orientation)

- ❑ Outdoor or recreational sports
- ❑ Physical Health
- ❑ Religious
- ❑ Residence Hall
- ❑ Student clubs and organization(s)
- ❑ Student government
- ❑ Student productions or media
- ❑ Study abroad
- ❑ Other (please specify): ____

Q16. What are the title(s) of the peer leader position(s) that you hold or have held: _______________________

Q17. You indicated you served in the following roles: (*Populate from Q15*). Indicate the time you served in each role. (*Only options chosen from Q15 will show*)

Type of Peer Leader Experience	Time in Role
(*Populated from Q15*)	❑ Less than 1 semester/term
	❑ 1 semester/term
	❑ 2 semesters/terms
	❑ 3 semesters/terms
	❑ 4 semesters/terms
	❑ 5 semesters/terms
	❑ 6 semesters/terms
	❑ 7 semesters/terms
	❑ More than 7 semesters/terms

Extent of Peer Leader Experience(s)

Q18. How many peer leader positions do you currently hold?

- ❑ 1
- ❑ 2
- ❑ 3
- ❑ 4
- ❑ 5 or more

Q19. What is the highest number of peer leader positions have you ever held at one time?

- ❑ 1
- ❑ 2
- ❑ 3

❑ 4

❑ 5 or more

Q20. Including any current positions, how many total peer leader positions have you held during your university experience?

❑ 1

❑ 2

❑ 3

❑ 4

❑ 5

❑ 6

❑ 7

❑ 8

❑ 9

❑ 10 or more

Q21. On average, how many hours per week do you spend performing your peer leader responsibilities?

❑ 5 hours or less

❑ 6-10 hours

❑ 11-15 hours

❑ 16-20 hours

❑ 21-25 hours

❑ 26-30 hours

❑ 31-35 hours

❑ 36-40 hours

❑ More than 40 hours

Q22. Have any of your peer leader roles included serving as a senior peer leader, supervising, or mentoring other peer leaders?

❑ Yes

❑ No

❑ I don't know

Q23. Using the slider below, please describe the extent to which your peer leader responsibilities were carried out online or in person.

Completely Online ——————————|—————— Completely In Person

How Peer Leader Experiences were Acquired

Q24. Which of the following best describes the peer leader selection process you went through?

Type of Peer Leader Experience	Time in Role
(Populated from Q15)	☐ I applied for, and was interviewed for the position/was subsequently appointed
	☐ I was nominated for the position (by another person) and subsequently appointed
	☐ I volunteered for the position and was subsequently appointe
	☐ I was elected to the position
	☐ Other selection process

Q25. What motivated you to take on your peer leadership role/s? Select all that apply.

- ☐ To help or benefit other students
- ☐ To share my knowledge/experience with others
- ☐ To give back to or serve the University
- ☐ For personal/professional challenges and skill development
- ☐ For academic development - improve my subject knowledge
- ☐ For current or future job prospects
- ☐ To earn an income while studying
- ☐ To receive reduced study/accommodation fees
- ☐ For the enjoyment/experience
- ☐ To be more involved in the University community, meet new people
- ☐ To be more involved in academic/governance aspects of the University
- ☐ Other (please specify): _______________________________________

Training

Q26. Did you receive initial training for your peer leader position(s)?

- ☐ Yes, for all of the peer leadership positions I have held
- ☐ Yes, for most of the peer leadership positions I have held
- ☐ Yes, for some of the peer leadership positions I have held (but not most)
- ☐ No
- ☐ I don't know.

Q27. How long was the initial formal training for your current and/or previous peer leader position(s)? (Select all that apply.) [*Display if Q26='Yes'*]

- ☐ Half a day or less

☐ 1 day

☐ 2 days

☐ 3 days

☐ 4 days

☐ 1 week

☐ 2 weeks

☐ 3 weeks

☐ My initial training required my enrollment in a mandatory class.

☐ Other (please specify): ____

Q28. Did you receive any additional ongoing formal training after the initial training?
[*Display if Q26 = 'Yes'*]

☐ Yes

☐ No

☐ I don't know

Q29. What type of additional ongoing formal training did you receive? (Select all that apply.)
[*Display if Q28 = 'Yes'*]

☐ Regular meetings specifically dedicated to training, such as workshops

☐ Periodic refresher sessions (e.g., prior to or during semester)

☐ Training during a retreat

☐ Training during staff meetings

☐ Training during meetings with supervisor

☐ Online or asynchronous self-paced training

☐ Other (please specify): ____

Q30. Were you provided with regular opportunities to receive feedback on your performance as a peer leader?

☐ Yes

☐ No

☐ I don't know

Q31. How was this feedback on your performance provided? (Select all that apply.)
[*Display if Q30 = 'Yes'*]

☐ Meetings with a supervising faculty or staff member

☐ Meetings with a senior peer leader

☐ Surveys, questionnaires, or evaluations completed by the students who you led

☐ As part of roleplay exercises, simulations, or mock teaching/advising sessions

☐ Other: (please specify): ____

Q32. Were you provided with periodic structured opportunities to reflect on, articulate, or integrate the learning you were experiencing as a peer leader?

- ❑ Yes
- ❑ No
- ❑ I don't know

Q33. What type of opportunities for reflection and integration were you provided? (Select all that apply.) [*Display if Q32 = 'Yes'*]

- ❑ Regular conversations with a supervising faculty or staff member
- ❑ Regular conversations with a senior peer leader
- ❑ Group discussions during training meetings with other peer leaders
- ❑ Written reflections (e.g., journals, weekly reports, end of semester reports)
- ❑ A portfolio containing artifacts and reflections demonstrating the knowledge and skill developed as a peer leader
- ❑ Other: (please specify): ____

Compensation

Q34. What compensation did or do you receive for your work as a peer leader? (Select all that apply.)

- ❑ I volunteer as a peer leader and do not receive any compensation.
- ❑ Acknowledgement on academic transcript
- ❑ Course credit
- ❑ Financial compensation such as an hourly wage or a stipend
- ❑ Financial aid such as a scholarship
- ❑ Reduced tuition or fees
- ❑ Room and board reduction
- ❑ Gift cards, vouchers, or other gifts
- ❑ Other (please specify): ____

Effects of Peer Leadership Experience(s): Outcomes

To what degree have the following *skills* changed as a direct result of your peer leadership experiences?

Skills	Greatly Decreased	Decreased	Slightly Decreased	No Change	Slightly Increased	Increased	Greatly Increased	Unable to Judge
Q35 Academic								
Q36 Critical thinking								
Q37 Time management								
Q38 Organizational								

Skills	Greatly Decreased	Decreased	Slightly Decreased	No Change	Slightly Increased	Increased	Greatly Increased	Unable to Judge
Q39 Project management								
Q40 Leadership								
Q41 Teamwork and Collaboration								
Q42 Interpersonal communication								
Q43 Written communication								
Q44 Presentation								
Q45 Problem solving								
Q46 Decision Making								
Q47 Adaptability								
Q48 Creativity								

To what degree have the following *college or university experiences* changed as a direct result of your peer leadership experiences?

	Greatly Decreased	Decreased	Slightly Decreased	No Change	Slightly Increased	Increased	Greatly Increased	Unable to Judge
Q49 Your meaningful interaction with faculty								
Q50 Your meaningful interaction with staff members								
Q51 Your meaningful interaction with peers								
Q52 Your knowledge about people with backgrounds different than your own								
Q53 Your interaction with people with backgrounds different than your own								
Q54 Your understanding of people with backgrounds different than your own								
Q55 Your knowledge of campus resources								
Q56 You're feeling that you belong and are welcome at your institution								
Q57 Your desire to stay at your institution and graduate								
Q58 Your desire to engage in continuous learning following graduation								
Q59 You're feeling that you are contributing to your campus community								

To what degree have the following *abilities* changed as a direct result of your peer leadership experiences?

	Greatly Decreased	Decreased	Slightly Decreased	No Change	Slightly Increased	Increased	Greatly Increased	Unable to Judge
Q60 Analyzing a problem from new perspectives								
Q61 Creating innovative approaches to complete a task								
Q62 Providing direction through interpersonal persuasion								
Q63 Sharing ideas with others in writing								
Q64 Building relationships with people with whom you work								
Q65 Engaging in ethical decision-making								
Q66 Bringing together information learned from different places								
Q67 Applying knowledge to a real-world setting through hands-on experiences								
Q68 Succeeding in a full-time job after graduation								

To what degree has each of the following *academic performance* areas changed as a direct result of your peer leadership experiences?

	Greatly Decreased	Decreased	Slightly Decreased	No Change	Slightly Increased	Increased	Greatly Increased	Unable to Judge
Q69 Your GPA								
Q70 The number of credit hours you have completed each term								
Q71 The time to your expected graduation								
Q72 Your overall academic performance								

Q73. How has being a peer leader affected your academic performance? (please describe)_______________

Training

Q74. Would you recommend being a peer leader to other students?

- ❒ Yes, absolutely
- ❒ Yes, for most of the peer leadership positions I have held

- ☐ Yes, for some of the peer leadership positions I have held (but not most)
- ☐ No
- ☐ I don't know.

Q75. How would you rate your overall satisfaction with your peer leadership experiences?
- ☐ Very dissatisfied
- ☐ Dissatisfied
- ☐ Slightly dissatisfied
- ☐ Neutral
- ☐ Slightly satisfied
- ☐ Satisfied
- ☐ Very satisfied

Conclusion

Q76. How did the COVID-19 pandemic impact your peer leader experience? _____________________

Q77. Is there anything else you would like to share about your peer leader experiences? _________________

Appendix C

List of Institutions Participating in the 2022-23 US Administration of the International Survey of Peer Leaders

Institution	City	State
Abilene Christian University	Abilene	TX
Brigham Young University	Provo	UT
California State University-Chico	Chico	CA
California State University-Fresno	Fresno	CA
Ensign College	Salt Lake City	UT
Furman University	Greenville	SC
Grambling State University	Grambling	LA
Kent State University	Kent	OH
Knox College	Galesburg	IL
Middlesex Community College	Bedford	MA
Ohio University	Athens	OH
Salt Lake Community College	Salt Lake City	UT
San Jose State University	San Jose	CA
Southern Utah University	Cedar City	UT
Triton College	River Grove	IL
University of Georgia	Athens	GA
University of New Hampshire	Durham	NH
University of New Mexico	Albuquerque	NM
University of South Carolina	Columbia	SC
University of Texas-Tyler	Tyler	TX
University of Utah	Salt Lake City	UT
Utah State University	Logan	UT
Utah State University-Eastern	Price	UT
Utah Valley University	Orem	UT
Virginia Commonwealth University	Richmond	VA
Washington University-St. Louis	St. Louis	MO
Weber State University	Ogden	UT

Appendix D

International Survey of Peer Leaders - US Participant Demographic Profile

Project Background

The following presents a demographic profile of the participants in the 2022-23 administration of the International Survey of Peer Leaders in the US. The profile presents a profile of all participants in the survey as well as those students who responded indicating that they currently or had at some point served as a peer leader role on their campus.

We share these data to provide an overall demographic description of the sample of participants, and we make no claims as to the representativeness of this sample for the entire population of peer leaders in the US. With future administrations and additional participation of campuses in the research, this profile will contribute to a further understanding of the demographic profile of the population of peer leaders on campuses in the US.

Participant Characteristics	All Respondents			Peer Leaders		
	N	Freq.	%	N	Freq.	%
What was your cumulative GPA at the start of the current term?	1484			1358		
0.00-0.50		5	0.3		4	0.3
0.51-1.00		0	0.0		0	0.0
1.00-1.50		0	0.0		0	0.0
1.51-2.00		3	0.2		1	0.1
2.01-2.50		27	1.8		24	1.8
2.51-3.00		116	7.8		109	8.0
3.01-3.50		339	22.8		303	22.3
3.51-4.00		994	67.0		917	67.5
What is your class standing (based on number of full-time equivalent years attended at any university or college)?	1531			1397		
First-year student		84	5.5		67	4.8
Second-year student		453	29.6		409	29.3
Third-year student		467	30.5		425	30.4
Fourth-year student		394	25.7		370	26.5

table continues on page 144

table continued from page 143

Participant Characteristics	All Respondents			Peer Leaders		
	N	Freq.	%	N	Freq.	%
Fifth-year student		85	5.6		82	5.9
Other		48	3.1		44	3.1
During the school year, which of the following best describes your housing?	1529			1395		
On-campus housing		577	37.7		523	37.5
Off-campus housing, sponsored by your college or university		127	8.3		116	8.3
Off campus housing, not sponsored by your college or university		825	54.0		756	54.2
Have any of your parents or guardians earned a four-year college degree?	1529			1395		
Yes		1159	75.8		1060	76.0
No		363	23.7		330	23.7
I don't know.		7	0.5		5	0.4
Are you eligible for financial aid under the Pell Grant program?	1528			1395		
Yes		476	31.2		434	31.1
No		677	44.3		623	44.7
I don't know.		375	24.5		338	24.2
What is your residency status?	1523			1397		
In-state student		982	64.5		911	65.2
Out-of-state student		478	31.4		431	30.9
International student		63	4.1		55	3.9
What is your age?	1524			1398		
Younger than 18		4	0.3		3	0.2
18-20		667	43.8		597	42.7
21-25		809	53.1		756	54.1
26-30		27	1.8		26	1.9
31-35		6	0.4		6	0.4
Older than 35		11	0.7		10	0.7
What is your gender?	1524			1398		
Agender		7	0.5		6	0.4
Man		408	26.8		364	26.0
Woman		1034	67.8		956	68.4
Nonbinary/Genderqueer/Genderfluid		54	3.5		52	3.7
Another identity not listed here		5	0.3		4	0.3
Prefer not to say		16	1.0		16	1.1
What is your race or ethnicity? Which of the following do you identify as? (Select all that apply.)	1522			1396		
American Indian or Alaska Native		15	1.0		11	0.8
Asian or Asian American		134	8.8		120	8.6
Black or African American		107	7.0		94	6.7
Hispanic, Chicano/a, or Latino/a		229	15.0		206	14.8
Native Hawaiian or other Pacific Islander		13	0.9		12	0.9

table continues on page 145

table continued from page 144

Participant Characteristics	All Respondents			Peer Leaders		
	N	Freq.	%	N	Freq.	%
White		1127	74.0		1043	74.7
Other		27	1.8		25	1.8
I prefer not to respond to this question.		20	1.3		18	1.3

About the Editors

Dr. Bryce D. Bunting is an associate clinical professor, the Assistant Dean of Undergraduate Education, and Director of the First-Year Experience at Brigham Young University (BYU). Bryce frequently presents at national and international conferences including the National Academic Advising Association (NACADA); NODA; International Society for Exploring Teaching and Learning (ISETL); NASPA; Association for the Study of Higher Education (ASHE); and the American Educational Research Association (AERA). Bryce also serves as an affiliate scholar and national advisory board member for the National Resource Center for the First-Year Experience and Students in Transition; as a member of the Editorial Review Board for the *Journal of The First-Year Experience & Students in Transition*; and is the former editor of the *Journal of Peer Learning*. His research agenda is focused on practical strategies for helping students adopt productive learning mindsets; using instructional design to inform the development of high-impact and transformative learning experiences in college; the impact of peer leadership on those who serve as peer leaders; and the application of learning theory to rethinking and redesigning college transitions. He was a peer leader as an undergraduate student and cites it as the most transformative thing that happened to him during college.

Dr. Dallin George Young is an assistant professor in College Student Affairs Administration (CSA A) and Student Affairs Leadership (SAL) at the University of Georgia. His research agenda includes using activity-based theoretical perspectives to interrogate student transitions into the academy; how graduate and professional students learn the rules, knowledge, and culture of their aspirational professional communities; and the impacts of educational structures on the success of these transitions, including investigating differential effects on student populations.